LEWIS HENRY MORGAN

Social Evolutionist

LEWIS HENRY MORGAN

Social Evolutionist

By BERNHARD J. STERN

NEW YORK / RUSSELL & RUSSELL

FIRST PUBLISHED IN 1931

REISSUED, 1967, BY RUSSELL & RUSSELL

A DIVISION OF ATHENEUM HOUSE, INC.

L. C. CATALOG CARD NO: 66—24763

PRINTED IN THE UNITED STATES OF AMERICA

CHAPTER I

THE LIFE OF LEWIS HENRY MORGAN

I

The life of Lewis Henry Morgan is that of a conventional middle-class "first-citizen" of the middle decades of the nineteenth century. These were years of restless activity of the rising capitalist class in the United States. Speculation was rife throughout the country; the romance of the expansion movement to the west gripped the imagination of possessors of capital eager to exploit the natural resources of this well-nigh untouched domain. The country was electric with the boom spirit; previously unheard-of fortunes were being accumulated. It was an era of triumph for business enterprise, a period of aggressive capitalist manipulation. The plodding, leisurely agrarian spirit of the half-century previous had given way to the hectic acquisitive spirit of a period of exploitive speculation.

Morgan was identified with, and did not rise above, the spirit of this era. In spite of any minor faults he might discover about their functioning, he never for a moment doubted but that capitalism was the best system, the United States the best democracy, and Christianity the only true religion in this better-than-all-previous worlds. He was not one of the avaricious, grasping, covetous individuals of which his era produced many. His essential humanness, combined with a sus-

1

picious attitude toward overspeculation, restrained him from becoming a victim of the money greed that infected and distorted most of the new rulers of America. To the Civil War and the political and economic issues which it raised, he reacted with the rabid hysteria of a war period. Genuinely honest but politically ambitious, he allowed himself to be used by unscrupulous politicians as a smoke screen for their corrupt acts. He permitted himself to yield to the religious fundamentalism of a dominant clergyman rather than to declare for the evolutionists whom he secretly indorsed and whose views set the pattern for his social evolutionary ideas. His many acts of sincere generosity and personal charity, which relieved the feeling that he may have profited at the expense of others, and his interest in popular education to train more efficient workers and develop a "new woman" to meet the needs of a rising capitalist society reflect the behavior of many of the more liberal members of the new American aristocracy of wealth.

For the purpose of this study, Morgan's personality and life-history are primarily important in affording the background and setting of his concepts and facilitating the interpretation of his writings. It will be seen that his biography throws in clear relief much that was previously obscure, and brings out in bright colors much that was dull gray. In the light of his biography many sentences in his books take on new meaning and many accents are shifted.

II

There was no nonconformist tradition in Morgan's background. He came from an "old New England fami-

PREFACE

The anthropological theories of Lewis Henry Morgan have had very wide influence. American, European, and Australian anthropologists have expressed indebtedness to his works; and sociologists and historians have used his evolutionary classifications. His book *Ancient Society* has become a socialist classic.

Controversies over the value of Morgan's contributions have persisted a half-century after his death. The present work discusses these controversies and aims to cast new light on the genesis and development of Morgan's theories and to evaluate them in the light of contemporary knowledge. The·author has made use of hitherto unconsulted manuscript materials which have facilitated his interpretation of Morgan's work in the setting of his milieu and of his personal history.

Grateful acknowledgment is made to Donald A. Gilchrist, librarian of the University of Rochester, for his co-operation in making these manuscripts accessible, and to the many others who have provided the author with materials dealing with Morgan's life and work.

BERNHARD J. STERN

TABLE OF CONTENTS

vii

ly" possessing all the qualities of temperament and cultural heritage traditionally associated with that designation. James Morgan had sailed from Bristol in the ship "Mary" in the summer of 1636 and had first settled at Sandy Point near Gloucester. Finding the coast bleak and the Indians troublesome, he moved to New London with the Sandy Bay Colony headed by the Rev. Rich Bluman, its pastor. In 1650 he had been assigned six acres of land and in 1662 was rated the third highest among the taxpayers, holding 250 pounds. His son was deputy general of the Court of New London. The next two generations were military men, the first John, captain of the Train Band of Groton, his son John, captain of the Fourth Company of Groton. Thomas, the sixth son of John, the grandfather of Morgan, moved in 1792 to become a farmer at Scipio, Cayuga County, New York, now Ledyard. Morgan's father, Jedidiah, moved from Ledyard to Aurora, Cayuga County, which was still a wilderness surrounded by Indians. Here Lewis Henry was born in 1818 as the ninth child of his father's thirteen, the fourth offspring of his father's second wife, Harriet Steele Smith, who also traced her antecedents back to the early English settlers. His father was elected state senator and died after three years in office, when Morgan was eight. All this stands related in the *History of the Family of Morgan from the Year 1089 to Present Times* by Appleton Morgan of the twenty-seventh generation of Cadevor-fawr, in the compiling of which genealogy Morgan, who gloried in his ancestry, had assisted avidly.

III

Morgan spent his youth in the sparsely inhabited region around Lake Cayuga near a settlement of Iroquois Indians, receiving the best elementary education then available in the rural districts of New York. He attended Cayuga Academy in Aurora preliminary to going to Union College. At Cayuga Academy, he first manifested his club-organizing proclivity which characterized him throughout life. His name heads the list of members of the Erodephicin Society, before which compositions were read; the outstanding feature of this organization was the assessment of fines of six and one-quarter cents and twelve and one-half cents against members who refused to deliver papers when requested. In 1838, he registered at Union College as a Junior, signifying that he was a Presbyterian and that all bills were paid by "himself." His records during his two years at college indicate the nature of a college education in this period, and Morgan's excellent grades in the limited courses offered are shown in the table on page 5.

When he returned to Aurora, he again attended Cayuga Academy, for one year, specializing in Latin and Greek; this training facilitated his researches later in life. He then read law until 1844, when he received a license to practice under the laws of the state of New York and became the law partner of George F. Danforth.

IV

As soon as the grave, serious-minded Morgan returned to Aurora from college, he tried his powers at public speaking. His choice of subjects varied: "Non-resistance," "Geology," "History and Genius of the Grecian Race," and his favorite "Temperance." Pompous, sententious, and oratorical, these youthful attempts none the less give us an insight into Morgan's

JUNIOR YEAR (1838–39)

	First Term	Second Term	Third Term
Attendance...............	99	98	100
Conduct.................	100	100	100
Trigonometry..............	98	....	....
Greek.....................	99	....	....
Rhetoric..................	99	....	....
Conic Sections.............	....	96	....
Cicero's *Orations*...........	....	98	....
Mechanics.................	....	98	....
Italian....................	....	....	99
Political Economy..........	....	....	99
Hydrostatics...............	....	....	99

SENIOR YEAR (1839–40)

Attendance...............	94	Absent	....
Conduct..................	100	....	....
Introductory Philosophy....	98	....	....
Optics....................	100	....	....
Kames and Guigot.........	100	....	....
Law......................	....	....	98
Butler....................	....	....	98
Physiology................	....	....	99

cultural orientation and leanings, and in many places reveal the germs of his future discussions.

An address on "Geology" delivered in 1841, which resolves itself into an exposition of what the textbook contains, opens with a passage which might be considered a personal challenge to steel himself for future patient inductive inquiry:

The study of any science requires more of us than we are willing to allow; it requires a *"persevering industry"* in the examination of the facts, and an *"unwearied patience"* amid the perplexities with which all science is surrounded. Without these qualities our progress would be slow, and our attainments inconsiderable. Man is endowed with neither industry nor patience; they are entirely a result of cultivation, as their opposites are most frequently imbibed; but it is a curious fact that the more has been effected in the civilization of man by these two great virtues, than by all the other agencies combined. There is no great event, no reformation, no era in science recorded in the history of man, that has not been the result of that *"persevering industry"* and *"unwearied patience"* of which I am speaking. For they conquer who believe they can: *"Possunt quia posse videtur."*

Although Lyell had completed his epoch-making treatise in 1833, showing the evolution of the earth, through a study of its strata—a book later to affect Morgan's theories very pronouncedly—his fame had not yet percolated to the environs of this sober tyro who still discoursed on the conflicting Neptunian and Plutonian doctrines of Werner and Hutton. But discoveries of the antiquity of the world could not shake the youthful Morgan's faith in the Mosaic account of creation:

The Mosaic account of the creation declares that "in the beginning God created the heaven and the earth." From this it would first appear that the creation itself was a miracle, it precluded all enquiry into the manner of the formation of the earth. And elsewhere, "the earth was spoken into existence." But on the other hand, in the next verse it reads, "the earth *was* without form and void and darkness rested upon the face of the deep."

How long the earth continued without form, and in this chaos, we have no means of knowing. This then is the great *nil et* of the theories and speculations of which we have been speaking. (Mr. Comstock in alluding to this field for conjecture remarks: "We may believe without the least violation of the sacred text that the materials of which the earth is composed were created a thousand or a million years before they were brought into a form for the habitation of Man." Com. Geo. p. 315.) So ready is the mind of man to press through the smallest aperture in search of truth or to urge the explorations of science with the daring of genius almost to the beginning of time.

The passionate fervor with which Morgan participated in the temperance crusade reveals the intensity of the influence of his conservative religious and moral background, an influence from which he never emancipated himself. The twenty-five-year-old speaker castigated Demon Rum to a Scipio temperance audience (through which town more whiskey and beer was carted than any section of the state) with a vehemence that smacked of fanaticism:

This evil does not arise among men suddenly, like the tempest that uproots the oak upon the mountainside, carries desolation through the plain and then subdues never more to visit these places but rather like the fever, which proceeds gently at first acquiring strength with its progress and when the climax is reached and the final struggle takes place between it and the living principle it gains the victory and subsides only when life itself is extinct, upon which it preyed. . . . . I shall say nothing of the injurious nature of ardent spirits, of the force of habit, the degradation of our moral nature, the waste of property or the idleness of crimes engendered by their use in our communities. . . . . The history of other nations furnish us material of the calamities originated by intemperance and of its influence upon their decline and fall. Thus inciting us to redouble our desire of making this reformation complete and perpetual, that in after years the strength of our great and splendid republic may not be shaken or its prosperity be impeded by the ravages of such a national disease, but rather having cured this distemper in its earliest stages let the American republic, the only government ever instituted that has appreciated the dignity and independence of man, go down to posterity as pure and unsullied as it was created, an example to all nations of the earth, of all that is sound in morality, elevated in religion and noble in liberty. . . . . In the catalogue of national sins that have led to the overthrow of Grecian and Roman republics, I need not tell you that intemperance stood first and last upon the list; or that then as now it was the mother of nearly every other vice of idleness and crime, of dissensions and tumults, of folly and delusion, of suffering and misery, of assassination and robbery and of self and national debasement. . . . . How many cities have been captured and plundered while the people were engaged in riot and debauching. Did you not think of the Feast of Belshazzar as a striking example of national revel and the disasterous consequences that follow quick upon them?

Then followed a vivid description of the festival that must have made his drab repressed rural audience secretly long to have been there to participate:

. . . . All that art could conceive or luxury desire was there, even the air was fragrant with a thousand odors. Presently these gay votaries of pleasure assemble for the feast. . . . . Then rises the music of the lute and the dulcimer and all is mirth and festivity within. The wine circulates with more and more freedom and intoxication soon rouses the spirit of riot and profanity. . . . . It is nearly impossible to estimate the terrible condition of national morals in the later days of the Roman republic. They were not degraded by drunkeness alone but by every vice that human depravity could originate or criminal appetite indulge . . . . one thing is certain that vice can uproot every virtuous principle from the heart and leave man a mere frame, weak, dismantled, and disrobed of all attributes of Manhood. . . . .

Morgan was a total abstainer; and hard cider, the beverage made famous by the Whigs during the Harrison campaign of 1840, remained always the strongest drink served in his home. The only "vice" in which he ever indulged was the consumption of huge quantities of tobacco; and when he renounced smoking late in life, a friend wrote him: "I should as soon have expected the devil himself to partake of holy water."

V

Although Morgan had observed the Iroquois from early childhood, it was at this time that his serious work among the Indians had its inception, stimulated in a most bizarre fashion. He tells us in his diary that, though he had been admitted to the bar, he could not establish a practice "from the depression of all business." Having much enforced leisure, he became active in a literary club he had organized in Cayuga Academy, called the Gordian Knot, made up of a few "thoroughgoing" young men. Later they became enterprising, concluded to "cut the knot" and to change their organization to a secret Indian society modeled after the Iroquois, called the Cayugas, after the name of the tribe living near Aurora.

According to the account given by Charles T. Porter, a less-serious-minded charter member of the organization, and therefore a franker one, this group "effected a surreptitious entrance" into the building which a defunct Masonic lodge had built in Aurora, "attired themselves in the white robes of the officers and held there their initiations and harmless revels." They soon expanded their society by organizing "tribes" in neighboring cities; the Oneidas at Utica, the Onondagas at Syracuse, the Senecas at Waterloo, the Canan-daijia in Rochester and Lima, the Tuscaroras in Albion, and other Cayugas at Auburn, Ithaca, and Oswego. The fraternity was known under different names varying as knowledge of the Iroquois increased. It first took the modest name of the "Order of the Iroquois"; then the "Grand Order of the Iroquois," or *We-yo-Hao-de-ya-da-nah Ho-de-no-sau-nee;* finally, "The New Confederacy of the Iroquois," or *Ac-qui-nus-chi-o-nee,* signifying a united people. The ceremony of initiation, called "Inindianation," written by Morgan, indicates that the Order employed the typical mystery technique of secret societies to impress the new members with the supposed dignified solemnity of the occasion. The character of the society and its intellectual tone cannot better be portrayed than by a quotation from the concluding part of this ceremony which Morgan headed "Special Form of Inindianation Adopted at the Monthly Council of the Turtle Sachemship of the Senecas, Moon of the *Te-ah no-at-nah* 7th day, 1845":

Prophet

Young Warrior, you are about to take upon you the vows of a Seneca. It is a serious and solemn matter. It is a grave and solemn undertaking. We are not engaged in a trifling and transitory object but one of deep and absorbing interest and we do expect from you hereafter a vigorous and spirited assistance not only at our festivals, but also in our labors which are manifold and increasing. Do you promise to render it? [I do.] Do you also pledge yourself in the presence of the Great Spirit whose eye beholdeth us on this occasion; never to divulge the Secrets of our Order, which may be now or hereafter entrusted to your keeping? to preserve them in the spirit of rectitude and of honor, Yea with the Redman's faith? [I do.] Then as you heed this pledge will you be respected and trusted, and receive all our confidence; but on the other hand, if, in an idle hour, or with careless levity you should dare to lift the veil of Secrecy from our Order and expose it to the Pale-face, a *retribution* the very thought of which would make you shudder *even* in the *grave* will follow quick upon your erring footsteps. The Senecas never abandon a friend; neither do they ever forgive or forget an enemy or betrayer. But Young Warrior, we anticipate no evil from you, we have satisfied your claims to our fellowship, and we are satisfied that our confidence will be safely reposed. We give you a cordial welcome to our Council Fire and at all times hereafter, we shall greet you upon our hunting grounds as a brother and a Seneca.

Sachem Chiefs and Warriors of the Turtle Tribe of the Seneca Nation, do you receive him as an adopted warrior? [a War Chief].

[Ans. (The bandage is removed, the warriors standing in perfect silence and resting on their bows.) After a minute the prophet leads the novice towards the Sachem before whom he kneels—the Sachem then takes his hand with this grip:]

Sachem

This is the grip by which thou shalt know a brother. Mark it well. Thou shalt hereafter be known upon the War-path by the name of O-te-ti-an-i. Let thy conduct, enterprise, fidelity and zeal render this appelation renowned among the Seneca Warriors of the Genesee.

[The Sachem Prophet and the novitiate then stand together in the center while the Head Warrior leads the band around him in a march singing the war-song. After this is done the column stops, and the Sachem introduces each by his Indian name to the novitiate, who gives to him in turn the grip and their congratulations. This closes the ceremony. Next comes the address and poem, the business of the Council, refreshments, merriment, etc.]

The Grand Council· meetings of the society, held on the fourth Thursday in August each year, were special occasions of revelry and pageantry. Both the by-laws and constitution of the organization demanded that each member provide himself with a costume, and to these Grand Council meetings they came in full Indian regalia, with chaplets of eagle feathers, Indian tunics, scarlet leggings, and decorated moccasins. In the light of huge camp fires they listened to speeches and poems and derived amusement in the performance of the rites and ceremonies of the occasion. Their ardor was doubtless dimmed by an article in the constitution which read: "Believing that temperance and morality are essential to the well-being of the Confederacy, the use of Firewater in any way or manner is forever forbidden at all General or Special Councils of the Confederacy. . . . ."

A letter from Morgan to William L. Stone, author of

the *Life and Times of Red Jacket*, asking him to become an honorary member of the Order, reveals what Morgan conceived to be the serious purposes of the society:

I have the honor to inform you that at the Monthly Council of the Cayugas held on the 7th inst. you were unanimously elected as honorary member of the We-yo-Hao-de-ya-da-nah Ho-de-no-sau-nee or the Grand Order of the Iroquois. The order is composed of the Cayuga Nation, located at Aurora, numbering 65 members; the Seneca Nation at Waterloo in the County of Seneca, numbering 25, the Onondaga's at Syracuse numbering 20. The Tuscaroras in Albion numbering 10 and the Oneidas at Utica who have just commenced. The Mohawks yet remain to be instituted. It is now the third anniversary since the Order was founded in our place; and such has been our progress that we now have every expectation of building up and sustaining a flourishing valuable Indian Order.

We are young men but we believe we are engaged in a high and noble object: we have certainly a very beautiful and even magnificent foundation for an Indian Order and we now hope to enlist the interest and aid of those literary gentlemen of our Republic who have distinguished themselves in the field of Indian History and literature.

In our organization we follow the original Confederacy. Our Chief officer is a "Grand Tek-a-ni-ho-gea." In each Nation, our officers are a Sachem, a Hah-na-yo-oh or Prophet, a Har-yar-do-oh or Secretary, an Owistah or Treasurer and a Head Warrior. We also have a Council on the first Friday in each month, for an oration and poem, on which occasion we also initiate. We likewise have other meetings for business. . . . .

We need somewhere in our Republic, an Indian Order which should aim to become the vast repository of all that remains to us of the Indians, their antiquities, their customs, eloquence, history, literature, indeed, everything pertaining to them which can be rescued from oblivion to which it is rapidly hastening. Another of its leading objects should be to beget and encourage a kinder feeling towards the Red Man, a disposition to appreciate and render a just tribute of admiration to the many virtues of the Indian character; and above all, when the Order thus instituted shall have reached its full maturity, it should make the whole Indian race the object of its benevolence and protection: to shield them in their declining fortunes from oppression, and to mitigate to some extent the misfortunes which are hastening their dissolution.

Such an Order would have a vast and novel field of literary research, the romantic age of the western world; and surely the literary department of the Order would give ample range to the most gifted intellect. Indian life suggests ample materials for the philosophic, the poetic and the descriptive pen, and distant generations must look back to the Indian age for the fable, the antiquities and the romance of America. . . . .

The nature and object of our Order is of course secret from the world, and we rely with perfect confidence upon your honor as a gentleman to preserve it inviolate. . . . .

Henry R. Schoolcraft, then the outstanding Indian authority in America, in accepting the invitation to deliver the annual address at Aurora, wrote:

. . . . On the first blush the general object and aim struck me favorably. There is so much that commends itself to the right thinking and noble minds, in the remembrance of the Red Race, that I cannot hesitate to express my hearty concurrence in the plan of the proposed literary institution by the young men of western

New York. Ten thousand inspiring associations spring up to sustain it and if its plan and details are properly regulated and guarded by wisdom and guided by a true moral hand, I foresee nothing to prevent it from growing up to be one of the most beneficial and honorable institutions of the country. . . . .

The name by which I may be designated is "Alhalla."

P.S. The Iroquois were always governed in their movements by a prophet or priest and in your symbolic arrangements, their office should not be overlooked.

Salem Town, the other honorary member of the organization, was the author of a *System of Speculative Masonry*.

The preamble to the constitution of the society also written by Morgan and adopted, "on Sr-is-gak-nah 13, 1846," gives the best statement of the expressed purposes of the New Confederacy:

Believing that an institution of a literary and social confederation of the young men of our state, for the purpose of preserving all that remains to us of the Indians, their history, manners and customs, their government, mythology and literature; of creating and encouraging a kindlier feeling towards the Red Man, founded upon a truer knowledge of the virtues and blemishes of the Indian character; or rearing up an institution which shall eventually cast the broad shield of its protection and mantle of its benevolence over these declining races; of searching out, gathering and preserving the pioneer history of our state; and finally of promoting our own intellectual and moral improvement;— is an object both interesting and commendable: and believing also that the ancient confederacy of the Iroquois affords the most beautiful and comprehensive plan on which to establish such an organization:—we do order and adopt the following: . . . .

Morgan was the dominant spirit of the organization. He wrote its constitution and by-laws; determined its rites and ceremonies; and, above all, strove to give it dignity and purpose. It was in order to formulate the structure of the secret society after the pattern of the social organization of the Iroquois, and to get ideas for ceremonies and paraphernalia, that he made repeated visits to the Indian camps. Later he wrote in his diary:

We visited the Indians at Onondaga and at Tonawanda and at Buffalo, attending their councils from time to time, and making ourselves familiar with their conditions and their wants: but more particularly we engaged with ardor in the work of studying out the structure and principles of the Ancient League by which they had been united for so many centuries. We wished to model our organization upon this and to reproduce it with as much fidelity as the nature and objects of our order would permit. This desire on our part, led to the first discovery of the real structure and principles of the League of the Iroquois which up to that time were entirely unknown except in a most general sense.

His sojourns among the Iroquois, during which he was assisted by Ely Parker, a full-blood Indian, who acted as informant and interpreter, stimulated Morgan's keen interest in Indian life; and although he was not aware of their importance at the time, they determined his future work in ethnology. Morgan was not, therefore, a "born ethnologist, as his friend and co-worker, Adolph Bandelier, characterized him, but was made one by a secret society.

Morgan's work among the Iroquois was aided by the services he performed for the Seneca tribes in their litigation against the Ogden Land Company. The Senate of the United States, by a resolution passed June 11, 1838, through the connivance of the Ogden Land Company, had abrogated the unanimity principle of the Seneca, by authorizing a majority of their chiefs to make a treaty with this company for the sale of their lands in western New York. This company forced a treaty upon the Senecas under very questionable circumstances, as an investigation conducted by Morgan under the auspices of his New Confederacy proved. The Indians were opposed to selling their land, and therefore the company set aside $200,000 to secure the requisite votes of forty-one chiefs. Ten of the chiefs were paid $30,000 apiece; others were plied with rum until they were intoxicated, and then made to sign. Chiefs were made by sham elections and their signatures taken; while others signed the treaty as chiefs who were not so in fact, until the majority was obtained. Despite a long and angry controversy in which the Indians protested vigorously, the Senate finally ratified the treaty by one vote cast by the vice-president. The Indians refused to recognize the treaty; and since the government refused to execute it, a compromise was offered in 1842 by which two reservations were released from the operation of the treaty on condition that the Indians would sacrifice the other two, the Tonawanda and Buffalo reserves. The Tonawandas refused to give up their land, worth on an average of $16 an acre, to the land company for $1.67, and resisted attempts to dispossess them.

Authorized by the New Confederacy, which had set aside 30 per cent of its income for Indian welfare, and deputized to carry a memorial adopted by the citizens of Genesee County at a general convention on the subject called together at the instance of the society, Morgan went to Washington and was successful in exposing the methods of the company and securing the quashing of the treaty.

As a reward for these services, Morgan, Charles Porter, and another member of the New Confederacy were adopted into the group of Senecas living at Tonawanda during the corn harvest feast of 1846. Morgan was made a member of the Hawk clan, the son of Jimmy Johnson, the nephew of Red-Jacket, and was given the name *Ta-ya-da-o-wuh-kuh*, meaning "One Lying Across," which signified that he would serve as a bond of union between the Indians and the whites. This adoption facilitated his researches among the Iroquois. It must be mentioned, however, that contrary to the statement very often made when Morgan's researches among the Iroquois are referred to, Morgan never actually lived among the Indians for extended periods. His studies were made in a limited number of short visits to their reservations and by correspondence with Ely Parker.

Morgan, as the organizer of the secret society, sought to live up to the expressed purposes of the organization, not only by acting as the counsel of the Indians against the land grab, but by serving as intellectual dignitary at the Grand Council meetings described above. As Sachem Skenendoah, he delivered the "serious" addresses to the assembled members of the Order at the council meetings held in 1844, 1845, and 1846. He published them in 1847–48 in the *American Review: a Whig Jour-*

nal of Politics, Literature, Arts and Sciences (whose caption was "To Stand by the Constitution"), in the form of fourteen "Letters on the Iroquois, Addressed to Albert Gallatin, President of the New York Historical Society." These letters, with few interpolations and minor emendations, form Book I and parts of Books II and III of the *League of the Ho de no saw nee or Iroquois*, which was published in 1851. Book III also contains, practically unchanged, the reports on the articles which Morgan had gathered and described for the New York State Museum Indian Collection which had appeared in the museum reports of 1849 and 1850. Morgan thought that with the publication of this book his work with the Indians had ended. Later he wrote in his journal, "I laid aside the Indian subject to devote myself to my profession. My principal object in writing this work which exhibits abundant evidence of hasty execution, was to free myself of the subject."

VI

When Morgan moved to Rochester from Aurora in 1850, he had entrée to the homes of the "most desirable citizens." Anticipating marriage to his cousin Mary Steele, of Albany, he established a household on Fitzhugh Street, then known as the "ruffle-shirt ward" of Rochester. His possessions and interests at the time of his removal to Rochester are indicated by his will dated May 30, 1851:

Bequeath to sister Amanda my interest in the estate of my late father Jedidiah Morgan and pay her same as soon as same can be realized after the provisions of his will.

Residue to pay funeral expenses, residue divided into equal parts and turned into silver plate—one set to Amanda, other set to sister Harriette S. Porter.

Daguerrotype of mother, copy of Natural History presented me by State, gold chain and silver cross, moccasins presented by Mr. Parker and the Bible presented me by my mother to Mary E. Steele.

Copyright of *League of the Iroquois* (now valued at $750) give to my brother Hamilton when he is admitted to the ministry and not otherwise; provided he shall not sell it under ten years after my decease, but shall use the income and profits of the same or principal part thereof in purchase of books for his library. Also bequeath bookcase and books contained except the Natural History aforesaid. Use bookcase or give it to Amanda.

Brandt medal and Johnson Tomohawk to State of New York for museum. Medal value $300. Other articles (Indian) to Smithsonian Institution.

Office table to Charles Porter to take to New York and keep it. Otherwise sell proceeds with other effects.

I wish to be buried at Aurora beside my father.

If I marry all goes to my wife.

Morgan married soon after. His wife brought him in contact with no new tradition. Her ancestors had been among the first settlers of Hartford, Connecticut, the first of whom, John Steele, who had come to America in 1635, had been a member of the first council held in the state. From her early childhood she had been very religious, and her interest in church work and missionaries had convinced her family that she ought to marry a clergyman or a missionary. Morgan had to struggle to obtain the consent of her parents to his suit, and always felt proud of his conquest.

Mrs. Morgan, deeply religious as she was, had a con-

straining influence on Morgan's already not overimpetu-
ous nature. His love of whist, which led a friend to write
him, ". . . . I suspect that hair of yours which used to
bristle when you held three honors and seven trumps, is
getting somewhat thin on the top of the head," had to
be curtailed because his wife considered whist "worldly"
and unbecoming. She intensified his religious bent in
many ways; he offered no resistance.

It was Mrs. Morgan's practice to inscribe occasional
poetry to express affection for her husband. Morgan had
not a single book of poetry in his library except the Latin
classics (which came in a set). Such attempts as the
following were treasured and preserved:

Thy thoughts are haunting me.
O, there are words of low toned eloquence,
That sound within the heart more thrillingly,
Than the most joyous peals of music choirs.
We would hush horn and lute and singer's voice,
To list the melody that fills the *soul*.
We would listen on forever. Listen
Unmindful of the crowd that hovers round,
Of noisy mirth, of careless badinage;
Thoughtless alike of flying wings of time,
Of the moon hastening in her onward path,
Of stars that burn to ashes in the sky.
Thy thoughts are moving through my spirit now,
Like as on the face of waters moved One
Who changed the darkest·chaos into light.

Three children were born to Morgan and his wife—a
son, Lemuel, and two daughters. During one of Morgan's long trips, the children contracted scarlet fever;
the two girls died and the son, though he survived, was
ever afterward defective, a source of anguish not only

because of his condition but because his presence tended
to recall the girls to whom Morgan was deeply devoted.
The incident of their death was an emotional crisis in his
life from which he never recovered. It saddened his personality, which was already grave; it quieted his laugh-
ter, which was never boisterous. The dignified restraint
which had characterized his demeanor was enhanced by
the mask which shielded his inward sorrow.

VII

Immediately upon his coming to Rochester, Morgan
joined the First Presbyterian Church, of which he remained an active member until he died. He was an ardent and devoted board member, securing ministers for
the pulpit, having many clergymen as his week-end
guests, and regularly attending all church functions.
Religion was one of his prime interests: it dominated
all his researches, and he never emancipated himself
from his theological background. His early training, his
wife's interests, and, above all, his contacts with Rev.
J. H. McIlvaine, for many years minister of his church
and later professor of social science at Princeton University, buried deep any doubts or waverings he may
have entertained. McIlvaine, fearful lest Morgan's inquiries would lead him astray, took upon himself the
task of saving him for the church. Over a period of
twenty years he advised and exhorted him:

. . . . I am afraid that the sceptical writers, with
whom we are both so familiar, have not left you a simple
faith in Christ. Truly it seems to me that I see all around
these writers the moment they step out of their specialties, and begin to speculate on matters of faith, and I do

not hesitate to pronounce them all in whatever they have written in opposition to a simple and unconditional faith in Christ as the Master, or Teacher, and Revealer of the spiritual world shallow! shallow! shallow! The words of Christ reveal to my mind a depth and comprehension of the nature of man and of what constitutes his true well being, to which Herbert Spencer, Darwin, Huxley, Tyndall and the rest of them cannot make the least pretension. In their several scientific specialties I sit at their feet. . . . .

Although Morgan was not outwardly orthodox enough to satisfy McIlvaine, he was sufficiently sectarian to be accused of harboring a prejudice against Episcopalians; and a lifelong friend relates that she never knew him to show any temper excepting when she beat him at playing backgammon or when the Catholic church was mentioned.

It was undoubtedly out of deference to the pressure of McIlvaine, whose solicitude Morgan did not resent, as is shown by the fact that he dedicated *Ancient Society* to him, that Morgan nowhere in his books uses the word "evolution" or has a word of praise for the writers on this subject, although his works are permeated with their influence. When McIlvaine delivered Morgan's funeral oration, he announced his victory:

. . . . there is nothing in the most advanced results of our friend's investigations opposed to the Christian religion, or to our faith in the Holy Scriptures. Not a line or a word has he written, which in its bearings upon the Christian religion if he were here today, I could ask him to blot. In this sense he presents a striking contrast to the skeptical scientists with whom he was in constant correspondence and with whom his most intimate associations lay. For there are many of them, as you know, who fully recognised the value of our friend's researches who have hardly ever lost an opportunity of speaking disparagingly and even contemptuously of Christianity. Search through his writings and you will not find anything of the kind. Indeed it is a wonder to me that the closeness of his connections with these men produced so little of the effect upon his mind which might have been expected. I cannot say that it did not produce any effect, but of that I shall speak directly. He was brought e.g. into the closest relations with the most advanced advocates of the hypothesis of the theory of evolution as applied not only to human society and individual character, where all thinkers now recognize it but also to life and thought, regarded as evolved out of the possibilities, properties or endowments of dead matter. Our friend had not the least sympathy with this materialism into which the hypothesis may be and is often pushed. In proof of this statement, I need only mention that whilst his great work on "Ancient Society" was passing through the press, I called his attention to a passage which inadvertantly might have found its place there, and which might be construed as an indorsement of these materialistic speculations in connection with evolution, and he immediately cancelled the whole page, although it had already been stereotyped. . . . .

That Morgan was really sympathetic to the scientists as against clergymen in the acrimonious conflict that was going on during this period is revealed in his letter of commendation to the editor of the *Nation* of an article published just before *Ancient Society* appeared, entitled "Clergymen as Scientific Men." In this article the author vigorously challenged the competency of clergymen to pass judgment on scientific matters concerning evolution, in that their training was not in this field. Wendell Phillips Garrison's reply to Morgan's letter casts light on the sentiments which Morgan had expressed:

Mr. Godkin wrote the article on "Clergymen and Scientific Men." He has received a bushel of replies, but as I wrote to him the other day, the only way to meet them (as Huxley would meet them if he were to "let himself out") is to say outright that a theology resting upon an atonement called for by a supposed angelic creation of mankind and subsequent fall, must take the consequences of building on the ground of science. Either science is not competent to find out for itself the beginnings of man, or if it is, woe to any theories about those beginnings which may collide with its discoveries. No doubt in my mind that Darwin's works are the theological as well as the scientific event of the age. The proper persons to deal with him are the Paulists for though we should have had the myth of Adam and Eve without Paul, he was responsible for connecting it with the mission and career of Jesus, and our theology is really not Christian but Pauline. The Jews have got along with the myth very well without persecuting anybody.

I am glad that you are plying your axe at the root of that false growth. It must be done silently and indirectly for a while but I hope to live to see the time when the first chapter of *Genesis* will have no more defenders among intelligent beings than any of Ovid's *Metamorphoses.*

I am pleased to have a fresh ground of sympathy with you and yet hardly fresh, for your researches are just as convincing to me as Darwin's on man's humble origin.

About the same time, Morgan clipped and heavily underlined a newspaper account of Dr. Augustus Le

Plongeon's discoveries in Yucatan, in which the correspondent states:

I am even timorous to insinuate it, lest the believers in the chronology of the Bible who make the world a little more than 5800 years old should come down on me, and after pouring upon my humble self their most damning anathemas, consign me at the dictates of their sectarian charity to that place over the door of which Dante read—

"Per me si va tra la perduta gente. ...
Lasciate ogni speranza voi ch'entrate."

Morgan feared the anathemas of the ever insistent McIlvaine, who wrote him:

. . . . As for the development theory, depend upon it that its advocates have not yet produced a single proof of it such as can be rigorously regarded as scientific. I say this apart from all theological considerations. Descartes' hypothesis of vortices explained the phenomena of astronomy far more perfectly than the developmental hypothesis does of organic life. Yet it proved wrong. . . . .

His care not to offend his wife, and McIlvaine's influence, caused him to refrain from expressing his real sympathies in regard to evolution in *Ancient Society*. The concluding sentence of this book is an attempt to reconcile his researches and his faith:

Civilization might as naturally have been delayed for several thousand years in the future as to have occurred when it did in the good providence of God. Their [our precursors'] labors, their trials and their successes were part of the plan of the Supreme Intelligence to develop a barbarian out of a savage and a civilized man out of a barbarian.

His book was so satisfactory to McIlvaine that the latter wrote him upon receipt of his presentation copy of the book which was to make Morgan universally known as one of the founders and main proponents of evolutionary anthropology:

I think it a great work, and decidedly the strongest argument against the Darwinians and in favor of the permanent species that has ever been given to the world.

Morgan always had misgivings about the conflict between the results and implications of his researches and his religious faith. In 1880 he wrote to Rev. Lorimer Fison who was gathering material for him on the Fiji Islands, asking him whether he thought that the work they were doing "was detrimental to the true religion." A friend tells the story that once when Dr. Herrick Johnson, of the Union Theological Seminary, preached a sermon on "The Influence of a Christian Man," Morgan, walking home from the church, sighed and said, "How I wish I were just such a Christian." His friend assured him that he was. "I am afraid not, I am afraid not, I am far from being one," he responded, trembling violently with emotion.

It was undoubtedly partly Morgan's religious orientation that led him to be antagonistic to Herbert Spencer's work. Other traditionalists in America were opposed to Spencer on this ground, as is indicated by the letter of President Porter of Yale written at this time to William Graham Sumner, with whom Morgan seems never to have come in contact:

. . . . The freedom and unfairness with which it [Spencer's *Study of Sociology*] attacks every Theistic

Philosophy of society and of history, and the cool and yet sarcastic effrontery with which he assumes that material elements and laws are the only forces and laws which any scientific man can recognize, seem to me to condemn the book as a textbook for a miscellaneous class in an undergraduate course. . . . .[1]

Morgan appears to have had similar sentiments, although he also attacked him on other grounds, as well, in one of the clubs which he organized, called the Spencer Club, which met fortnightly to discuss Spencer's work. Morgan criticized Spencer in a letter to McIlvaine, to which the latter responded:

. . . . Nor have I read Spencer, not having a doubt but that he has proved himself as great an ass in the discussion of ancient society as you say. As for reviewing him I am doing greater work and cannot come down.

Morgan also wrote to Darwin in disparagement of Spencer's work; and the ever friendly Darwin, busy with his plants, replied in a letter dated July 9, 1877, from Down, Beckenham, Kent:

I thank you kindly for your very kind, long and interesting letter. I write in fact merely to thank you, for I have nothing else to say. I have lately been working so hard on plants, that I have not had time yet to glance at H. Spencer's recent work, and hardly to do more than glance at your last work. But I hope before very long to find more time. It is, however, a great misfortune for me that reading now tires me more than writing, that is, if the subject sets me thinking. I am as great an admirer as any man can be of H. Spencer's genius; but his deductive style of putting almost everything never satisfies me, and the conclusion which I eventually draw is that "here is a grand suggestion for many years' work."

[1] H. E. Starr, *William Graham Sumner*, p. 346.

Your last work must have cost you very much labour and therefore I infer that you are strong and well. I can assure you that I have by no means forgotten my short and very pleasant interview with you.

The religious views of Morgan colored his interpretation of the history of the family and caused him to declare of monogamy, "The whole previous experience and progress of mankind culminated and crystallized in this pre-eminent institution," and to conceive of promiscuity as the earliest stage of relationship between the sexes because it was the antithesis of monogamy. His religious views also impinged on other of his interpretations. In 1853, he wrote:

The last cause of the decline of Athens was the impurity of its religious system. Its civilization did not rest on a moral basis. It not only reposed its hopes of the perpetuity of the race upon the civilization of the intellect and sense of physical beauty, but its religion itself was utterly incapable of maturing and strengthening those moral elements which alone can bind society together with enduring power.

Twenty years later Morgan expressed alarm at changing mores and morals and held that degeneration similar to that of ancient Roman times was imminent.

VIII

When Morgan came to Rochester, he became friendly with, and associated in financial enterprises with, Samuel P. Ely, who remained his financial adviser until he died. His meager resources soon grew. With Ely and a few other capitalists, he financed the construction of, and was a member of the Board of Directors of, a railroad which opened up the south shore of Lake Superior, rich in iron ore, and then an uninhabited wilderness. Morgan, from 1855 onward, made repeated visits to supervise the construction of the railroad. In 1858 the railroad was completed to the three principal iron locations, and in 1865 to Lake Michigan after an expenditure of about one and one-half million dollars. Morgan also acquired holdings in the iron mines. He had retired from active legal practice to oversee the construction of the railroad, and it and the mines were a profitable source of income. After the panic of 1873, with the falling-off of the demand for iron, his income declined. He lost some money also at this time in one of Ely's enterprises, and for this reason the latter was particularly solicitous of Morgan's investments. That Morgan suffered less from the panic than did many others is seen from the following letter from Ely dated November 20, 1875:

Your letter of 17th inst. with check of $1000 at hand. Received former letter with first $1000. I find that there are a number of small holders of both Superior and Ontenagen Co. stock who, being forced to realise by the pressure of the times, are selling for what they can get. I advise these people not to sell, but if they say they must have the money and dispose of some of their small blocks to speculators—when the speculator comes along I get his as cheaply as I can. I have picked up in this way several hundred shares at from $4 to $7 and I will put your money into this. The Cos. will not sell at any less than $10. I will average up a lot of Ontenagen and Superior so that you will get somewhere near 700 shares for the $4000 which you intend to put in. You are the only one out of all my old constituency who has put a dollar into my new enterprise . . . . and I am desirous that your unabated confidence in me (by which it is not too much to say I am deeply touched) should prove to be amply justified by the favorable result of the investment. . . . .

But the adventurous Ely, always prospecting in new mines, never totally regained the confidence of the more timid Morgan, who repeatedly suggested, against the protestation of the former, that his friend was the type through whom panics are bred. His losses in the disasters of 1873 had made Morgan fearsome about further investments. It was probably a rationalization of this fear which made him declare that a "mere property career is not the final destiny of mankind." In spite of his losses, Morgan's estate was over $100,000 when he died.

It was doubtless due to his economic orientation and his wealth that Morgan was entirely oblivious to the conditions of the workers in America in his day. He either did not know or sought to disregard the conditions revealed by Commissioner Well's report that the majority of workers had actually suffered a loss from the economic changes after the Civil War in the midst of the unparalleled accumulation of wealth by the capitalists. That he did not comprehend the significance of the industrial revolution taking place about him is revealed in the naïve remarks excerpted from an unpublished address delivered about 1876:

. . . . every citizen can leave the Republic whenever he chooses. And its whole tendency being to ameliorate the condition of the lowest of the community, I can hardly see why there should be any poor in the United States, except such as may be poor from misfortune, or owing to causes where the blame rests entirely with themselves. I speak of the poor as those needing the very sustenance of life, and have no shelter from the storm. For there is not one, I care not how low his circumstances may be, who has health, but can somewhere purchase an acre of ground, and draw his support from the soil. If he cannot pay outright he has credit; and a little industry and perseverance will soon place him above actual want. One day's labor in seven will support him, and three days' labor himself and his family. Yet there are none of this class of poor except in the cities; and I think on examination that most of these are foreigners, whose habits have become formed from modes of life in their native land, or the idle and dissolute, whom we may pity yet who deserve no compassion. For the American is not reared in dependency, and rarely if ever is improvident. When therefore I hear complaints from the more indigent of my countrymen, whose situation curiosity has led me to inquire into, that they can get no employment, I regard it only as an idle pretext.

In 1852, when the young Morgan, coming to Rochester, had not yet invested in mines and railroads and had not forgotten his own period of unemployment "due to the depression of all business," he was a bit more conscious of the problems of the workers. In a speech before the Rochester Athenaeum and Mechanics Association he declared:

There is an inherent tendency in property to accumulate into masses which when strengthened by partial legislation works out infinite mischief to the people. *Capital* and *labor* are two independent powers bound together by natural ties but usually standing in opposite ranks. *Capital* is very apt to encroach on *labor* and to seize every opportunity to dictate to *labor* its terms. Capital has sharp perceptions and thrifty cunning, while labor is unsuspecting and frequently in necessity. In every government, legislation should watch over the unprotected interests of labor; curbing at the same time the avaricious and hungry appetite of *capital*. . . . . Capital is the fund out of which labor must be paid and labor is the investment out of which capital draws its profits. No government is worthy of the name which suffers capital to reduce labor to dependence; to force from it by necessity that which it could not yield uncoerced. It makes no difference whether the victory is secured by general institutions or by the power of combination. Capital and labor should be equally independent to make such a contract as would be just and beneficial to both. But unfortunately capital has the surest fortune. It can rest when labor must be busy; it can contrive when labor is often writhing in destitution. As the world has been governed it is not surprised that capital has always gained the victory and held labor in its servitude.

His solution, which reflected the attitude of his class, was to make every laborer a small capitalist. This he conceived as being realized in the United States:

. . . . There will always be an unequal distribution of property. It is a necessary and unavoidable consequence. So also the greater the amount of wealth the larger will individual fortunes become. But favor the distribution of property to such a degree as to make labor essentially independent and then this inequality ceases to be important. We have already begun to realize largely one of the crowning blessings of our institutions, that they throw capital into the hands of labor, and thus ennoble it with freedom.

. . . . If our fathers had desired, above all other things, that we should become the richest people of the earth, they could not have framed any institutions better calculated than our own to produce this result. History and experience, both teach us that labor, in all the ages of the world, has been inhumanly defrauded. Industry when coupled with high sagacity has been sufficiently successful, but when coupled with the ordinary sagacity of the mass of the people, it has universally suffered. It has been despoiled primarily by civil institutions and then delivered over to the rapacity of capital for the consummation of the work. What has filled our marts with merchandise, our granaries with abundance and the world with wealth? Labor has done it. It would be natural to think that labor which has created all these means of enjoyment could rightfully claim the first provision. But we know the impressive fact that the people have toiled from generation to generation, from century to century, yet from first to last, industry has usually been clothed in rags while laziness has been robed in purple and linen. Rest assured society cannot be righteously organized when it yields such fruits. Our country is the only one on the face of the earth whose institutions have been so adjusted as to secure labor a manly stimulus and a just reward. . . . .

Then he revealed the ultimate purpose of his advocacy of diffusion of capital:

When the crisis of our fate as a free Republic shall arise, it will be found that the freeholders in this country who consist principally of farmers, mechanics and day-laborers will be the preservers of our institutions and the defenders of our liberties. Freeholders never make a mob, never repudiate the law, or annul the great principles of morality. . . . .

Finally, lest he offend the capitalists of Rochester, he concluded:

.... I shall not be understood to advocate any arbitrary division of property or any agrarian doctrine. All that is contended for is that labor shall have a fair and equal chance secured to it by equal and impartial laws and institutions. Such laws and institutions as we now have shall be preserved in all their spirit and improved by the lessons of experience.

Through Morgan's writings from the first in 1843 to the last in 1880, ran the theme of contrast of American republican institutions with those of the aristocratic institutions of Europe, a note prominent in all political speeches of his period and still heard in echo. Morgan seems to have glimpsed the fact more than did most of his contemporaries that the absence of an aristocracy was being glorified because it left the rising bourgeoisie in America unrestrained and unhampered in its frenzied rush for power and property. In the rise of this class, he exulted:

.... The luxury of that [the feudal] period would be barbaric ostentation in this; their civilization would be rudeness now. Commerce and manufacture have mainly produced the change. They have erected the great cities of the earth, constructed vast public works, supported armies and navies, filled the world with the humming notes of industry and raised nations to greatness. The first fruits of commerce and manufacture was the creation of a class of men who stood midway between the nobility and the people usually called the Middle Class, but in every just sense the first class in the nation which gave them birth. Raised to independence by profits of industry, and to respectability by the possession of wealth, they soon became the champion of popular rights. . . . . Great Britain owes this class all the liberty she possesses and which she so much vaunts, and we owe to it both the germ of our institutions and our Pilgrim fathers. The achievements of this class furnish some of the brightest pages of human history. Our fathers when they founded this Republic and the free states of which it is composed understood perfectly well the grievous abuses of the old governments of Europe and the institutions by which they were engendered and perpetuated. Hence they swept away in the first instance hereditary sovereignty and substituted a representative democracy. They abolished privileged classes and established equality.

But his stress on equality became dim as, with the passing of the years, Morgan saw an aristocracy of wealth in America take the place formerly held by the aristocracy of birth in Europe. As a member of this aristocracy, Morgan rationalized the existence of this class as being due to variations in intellectual equipment:

. . . . He [the observer] knows that property cannot be equally divided, and there must be an aristocracy of wealth, that God hath not given intellect to all men alike, and there is an aristocracy of talent; that some are endowed with more life energy and spirit than others and there must be an aristocracy of nature. . . . .

The critic of aristocracy of Europe had become the apologist of aristocracy of America. But mention of the glories of "democracy" is found as frequently as ever in his writings; he seemed little aware that his phrases sound like empty rhetoric. In *Ancient Society* he still inveighed against aristocracy—even of wealth—but saw no evidence of privileged classes in the United States.

IX

On one of his trips to the Lake Superior region on business connected with his railroad, in 1858, Morgan visited the reservation of the Ojibwa Indians and to his utter astonishment found that they possessed the same system of tracing relationship that he had found and considered so extraordinary among the Iroquois. His great idea was born, later to became almost an *idée fixe*, that "this method of tracing relationship was once universal." He later directed his energies with indomitable persistence in following up this clue, and from it he developed his famous contributions to ethnology: *Systems of Consanguinity and Affinity of the Human Family.*

It was also in the course of these trips that Morgan made his researches into the habits of the beaver that led to his book *The American Beaver and His Work.*

X

During the Civil War, the otherwise gentle Morgan was passionate in his enmity to the South. In 1862, in a memoir to Calvin Hudson, Jr., who had died at thirty-nine from an illness contracted during incarceration in a Confederate prison, he declared vindictively:

. . . . That this rebellion is to fall to pieces and the South again become loyal to the union, I do not believe. The alienation of her people appears to be absolute and total and we should accept it as a fact. We have grown asunder in the very elements of national life. The magnitude of the rebellion and the fires of hatred which now glow throughout the south are proof sufficient to the most incredulous. The Unity of our race is broken, it is broken by the infidelity of the South to the constitution, to the ties of kindred and to the great destiny which awaited us as a united people. Conscious inferiority superinduced by the curse of slavery is the originating cause of this mad attempt to hide themselves under the shelter of a Southern Empire. The earlier we accept these proofs the quicker will come our redemption. . . . . Upon this should our whole attention be concentrated. The rebels against our government have forfeited by one act of folly and of crime their privileges, their country and their homes, and should be expelled by the strong arm from every inch of American soil. . . . . This war should be waged until the very roots of this rebellion are extirpated and trodden under foot. . . . .

When Jefferson Davis was captured, Morgan urged that he be disfranchised and perpetually banished, demanding that he be sent forth

. . . . a sentenced and condemned criminal with the brand of Cain upon his forehead and representative at once of the conscious power, the mercy and the contempt of the American people. Shunned and despised by all honorable men, execrated by the many people whom he misled and betrayed and spared (from death) on their account and not on his own, his punishment and disgrace and miserable future life will be a warning to future generations.

In the acrimonious controversy which ensued after the Civil War, Morgan supported the "radical" plundering Reconstruction policy of Congress against the "moderate" policy of President Johnson, and was elected state senator on this platform.

XI

Morgan was elected Republican assemblyman from Rochester in 1861. The assembly record reveals nothing outstanding in his career as assemblyman, although his name appears repeatedly, his main work being that of chairman of the Committee on Indian Affairs. When he was nominated in 1867 for state senator, however, the *Rochester Union and Advertiser*, the Democratic paper, attacked him vigorously on his record. In an editorial comment on his nomination it declared:

His nomination, if he is elected, is to be regretted by all who have any regard for the interests of the district. He is a man of some literary qualifications, but as a legislator, he is deficient as he proved on a former occasion when sent to the Assembly. [October 9, 1867.]

Three days later, in an article headed "L. H. Morgan— Is He a Fit Man for Legislator," the newspaper was more specific:

First, he is a candidate and if elected will be a pliant tool of the clique of Lobbyists and Rottens who own and run the Rochester Democrat. . . . . His vote and actions both will be powerless in the accomplishment of any good. Of this we have practical proof in Morgan's career in the Winter of 1861 in the Assembly. In that body, when there was a Republican majority of 58, Mr. Morgan made himself a laughing stock. . . . . The bare fact of his advocacy of any ordinary measure about which the majority of the members are not fully posted was sure to kill it. . . . . We repeat Mr. Morgan only six years ago showed himself in the Assembly of the State as Representative of the city the most incompetent and worst failure of a member that can be found in the history of that body. . . . .

The *Rochester Democrat*, a Republican paper, had admitted, in its issue of October 10, that Morgan was unpopular with some of his party in the assembly, ascribing that fact to Morgan's active and unqualified support of Congress' Reconstruction policy.

The *Union* countered bitterly:

. . . . Morgan was unpopular because he made himself personally not politically offensive. His vanity was such that he wanted to see his name figure in the published reports of proceedings and he was constantly popping up in his seat and making motions etc. and pursuing such a ridiculous course that the whole House irrespective of party voted him an unmitigated nuisance.

On October 15, a letter appeared in the *Union* signed by "An Out and Out Republican":

Morgan is the tool of Brown. Brown is a notorious legislative lobbyist and Morgan will be mere putty in his hands. His ignorance and stupidity render him fit capital for Brown to trade upon.

The *Union* also declared in its issue of October 18 that a Committee of Republican common councilmen visited Albany in 1861 to get some charter amendments and found that they would be defeated if Morgan moved or supported their measure. By strategy they succeeded in getting Morgan out into the cloakroom while the measures were moved and passed. This ridicule of Morgan was ignored by the *Democrat;* but the *Express*, the other Republican paper, denied it emphatically.

Morgan's staunchest supporter for election was the *Rochester Democrat*, the leading Republican paper owned and edited by D. D. S. Brown. The paper refers to a speech which Morgan had made at the Pittsford Republican Convention, in which address Morgan had denounced President Johnson as a traitor, richly deserving impeachment, but had declared himself not unreservedly in favor of impeachment, feeling that such a procedure might endanger the Republican party and the welfare of the country by giving the Democrats an opportunity to raise a cry of revolution. The *Democrat* declared this speech to be characterized by "sterling Republican principles" and that it "evidenced Mr. Morgan's familiar understanding of the spirit and movements of the great Republican party." It further proclaimed Morgan to be "a gentleman of the highest standing and most spotless reputation. He is sound and true on all the great issues of the day. He is a supporter of the Congressional policy of Reconstruction and on the Central Railroad may be expected to uphold the interests of his constituents." It then printed some formal indorsement of other Republican newspapers of the state.

The support of the *Express* was more a matter of party conformity. It attempted to deny Morgan's affiliation with Brown, but this became increasingly difficult as the campaign progressed because the *Union* cited Morgan's visits to Brown's office. Finally, as a last defense, the *Express* resorted to the claim that Morgan, in spite of everything, was preferable to the Democratic candidate. During the last few weeks of the campaign the constant refrain of the *Democrat* was, "Nothing could be more beneficial to our candidate, Mr. Morgan, than the continued attacks of that scurrilous and mendacious sheet, the *Rochester Union and Advertiser.*"

Morgan finally won the election by a vote of 8,626 to 8,551, a bare majority of 75, which was out of proportion to other Republican majorities in Rochester, which ranged from 450 to 750.

During his term in the senate, Morgan voted always along party lines. It was during this session that a bill was insistently brought forward to provide for an investigation into the payment of graft by the Erie Railroad to various senators. Morgan voted against this bill until the final vote on April 10, 1868, when he changed his vote along with other senators. The following excerpt from the senate record then tells its own story:

Mr. Odell moved the following resolution:

Resolved: "that the select committee appointed to investigate the affairs of the Erie Railway be and they hereby are requested to hold their sessions in the Senate chambers and with open doors."

Mr. Murphy moved to amend as follows: "Or in some public room in the City of New York."

Mr. Morgan offered the following as a substitute: "That the resolution appointing a committee to investigate the affairs of the Erie Railway Company is hereby rescinded."

In the investigations which followed the passage of the bill, D. D. S. Brown, Morgan's strongest backer, was found to be implicated in the corruption. Morgan, however, appears not to have been involved in the scandals exposed. A few years later a fellow-senator, A. W. Palmer, from Amenia, wrote him:

The result of the late election would give such fellows as we are, a little more courage and a little better chance to "battle for the right." How those thieves used to run over us in 68 and 69. Our humiliating position was my reason for not accepting the renomination. . . . .

Morgan sent a letter of congratulation to J. H. Ramsey, of Albany, for his work in prosecution of the participants in the railroad scandal. The latter responded:

As a matter of duty and to rid the State and nation if possible of the disgrace brought upon us by the desperadoes Fisk and Gould, I intend they shall be brought to justice. The evidence can be adduced to showing they have issued over $35,000,000 convertible bonds without authority of the law or even the vote of the directors of the Erie Company, and what is worse have converted the avails amounting to millions of dollars to their own personal purposes. The conduct of these men will be looked upon as one of the wonders of the age.

Morgan was defeated in the nominating convention of 1869 by a candidate from the rural districts of the western part of the county.

His political life did not end with his defeat. He sought at once to secure an appointment as ambassador to Sweden from President Grant and urged all his political and scientific friends to solicit the president in his behalf. Among those whose aid he requested was that of John Norton Pomeroy, who responded:

. . . . The more persons the Government sends across like you the better it will be for us. I get more and more every day to hate the professed professional politician. I hope you are not doing for Fenton for Senator. For God's sake don't give the State of New York that prince of mere county politicians as our Senator.

Morgan was unsuccessful in his efforts to secure the post, and again failed in his application for ambassadorship to Spain in 1872, and to Italy in 1877. Though perhaps tempted, he appears never to have wanted to try state senatorship again.

Morgan was an ardent admirer of General Grant, whom he supported for president against Horace Greeley. In 1875, a friend from Michigan wrote him:

.... I have no doubt that you are now heartily sick of the national scourge called the Grant party. Of course you blush and apologize for voting for the old companion of the Digger Indians. But as you feel badly about it that is enough. You must join Sheridan's "banditti" and get punished for past sins.

Morgan never withdrew his support of Grant, even after the bungling inefficiency of the latter's administration had been exposed.

XII

Morgan's interest in promoting popular education began early in his life and continued until he died. One of his first legal tasks in Rochester in 1850 and 1851 was that of securing the provisional, and later the full, charter of the University of Rochester. He at once started a movement, which proved unsuccessful, to establish a "female college" or "female seminary" in conjunction with the University, to which project he returned repeatedly and for which he finally willed his money to the University. At the first commencement of the University of Rochester, an honorary degree of Master of Arts was conferred upon him as "lawyer and ethnologist." He later received an LL.D. from Union College.

Morgan often agitated for a project which he set forth first in 1850 for a permanent organization patterned after Cooper Union in New York City, to give free lec-

tures "for the mechanics and workingmen of Rochester
. . . . upon mechanical arts and upon the industrial and
economical questions of the times." Andrew D. White,
president of Cornell University, once wrote to Morgan
indicating that he was sympathetic to such extension
courses, in a letter dated October 22, 1868, from Ithaca:

Your paper [on the "Classificatory System of Relationships"] read before the Amer[ican] Acad[emy]
reached me yesterday. I have gone through it hastily
and reserved it for more careful reading.

Its thoroughness and extent have astonished me. It
seems hardly credible that one so engaged with cares
and duties of business and politics could find time for an
investigation so elaborate and philosophical and I desire
to thank you for finding such time and using it so ad-
mirably.

My reading this paper has revived my old wish that
we may at some time have the benefit of your work
here. While we carry out to the fullest extent the ideas
of our charters I am exceeding anxious to have the institution take more and more a University character, to
group men interested in pushing all leading branches of
knowledge and to bring to bear upon them just such
efforts as these of yours.

I believe that the effect of this, even upon our special
courses and departments would be excellent, giving
breath and depth to all.

We have an example of this now, though we are in the
rough, subject to many inconveniences and some priva-
tions, and the great majority of our students are of the
first year. The lectures of Prof. Agassiz are taking strong
hold of them. They are in some respects above them,
but they raise the tone of the whole institution and
Prof. Agassiz declares himself astonished at the thought
shown in the questions addressed to him by these young

men who under the system generally in vogue would be debarred from such lectures or would have science diluted or let down to their supposed level.

All this gives me hope that with advanced classes in the next two or three years we can have a higher and better sort of lectures in general, than such young men have generally been brought to listen to, and allow me to express the earnest hope that you will begin to throw the results of your various investigations into such a form that they can be brought to bear upon the more earnest students in our Universities and Colleges.

Under our system of Non-resident Professors which I firmly believe is to be largely adopted by the larger institutions, you would have a noble field both here and elsewhere.

And let me say in addition, that I have not forgotten your idea of sending out lecturers to act directly upon large classes of active men prevented from entering formally an University.

I believe that we are already beginning to train such and hope that the day is not far distant when our men may be seen in the centers of mechanical activity, and in the conferences on the Agricultural interest, practically and scientifically building up these two great branches.

Morgan, sensitive to his limitations, thought teaching "a mean business." He declined all amiable feelers that he should don a mortar board and gown and impose boredom on the young. He served as a member of the Board of Trustees of the University of Rochester and of Wells College and initiated several plans for scholarships for poor students in the face of the opposition of some of his reactionary friends.

XIII

In 1871 after his book *Systems of Consanguinity* had appeared, Morgan made a trip to Europe. He seems to have observed Europe with that dry literalness and grave earnestness that served him well when studying the habits of the beavers and the material culture of the Iroquois but which missed the aesthetic aspects of the life of Europe not yet Americanized by the tourist traffic and mechanized by giant power machinery. He sent two articles to his friend, Robert Carter, of *Appleton's Journal*, which articles rivaled modern Baedeckers in their elimination of the author's personality and in their pedantic exposition of fact. Carter acknowledged the receipt of these articles:

You attach, my dear friend too much importance to your articles especially to their illustrations. The articles are very good because you are an able man but if you were as familiar as you ought to be with modern literature, you would know that Venice and Heidelberg have been done to death with pen and pencil and that every large bookstore in our great cities is overstocked with works with illustrations in the finest style. . . . . You might have given them real value by giving the impressions of a man of the West by a new insight and scenes. What I wanted was your impressions and reflections on Oxford and in them, you will see, you fall into several blunders as was but natural. . . . . Harpers will not even look at them, I am sure, unless you can get a revolution or an earthquake at those places. Now if you will only give up your notion of illustrating places that have been illustrated ever since the art of engraving was invented and just use your Yankee eyes to see and describe things as they are in Europe, or as they seem to you, you might do something worth having.

When Morgan was in England, he made friendly visits to Charles Darwin and John Lubbock. A letter from Darwin, dated June 7, 1871, Down, Beckenham, Kent, indicates that his visit to Darwin was brief due to the latter's weak physical condition:

I shall have great pleasure in seeing you here on any day which will suit you; but please do inform me before hand. The best route is to leave Charing Cross by the 11:15 train for Orpington Station S. E. R. which is 4 miles from my house; and you will arrive here a little after 12:30. We will lunch at one o'clock and you can return by the 2:20 train. It grieves me to propose so short a visit, but my health has been very indifferent during the last week, and I am incapable of conversing with anyone except for a short time. I shall have great pleasure in seeing you . . . . .

Morgan's visit established a cordial friendship between the two men that was prolonged through correspondence. When Darwin's sons came to America, they carried letters of introduction by Morgan, as Darwin's letter of June 14, 1872, reveals:

I really do not know how to thank you for your extraordinary kindness in having taken such trouble for my sons. Your instructions about their route and your splendid supply of introductions will be invaluable to them. . . . .

Morgan, who had repeatedly expressed his antipathy to the Catholic church, nevertheless followed the tourist pattern and secured an audience with the pope, when he came to Rome. Later, Morgan, with a feeling of pride, related the tale that when the pope extended his hand to be kissed, Morgan addressed him, "Your honor, in

America we do not kiss a distinguished man's hand, but we shake it." The pope responded: "We will follow the American custom." Democracy had conquered theocracy!

When Morgan returned to America, he was glad to get back; he declared he had missed his apple pie.

XIV

It is in his championing of the cause of the harassed and exploited Indians that Morgan revealed his finest sentiments. His conflict with the Ogden Land Company and the purposes of his youthful secret society made a deep impression on him and led him to declare vigorously in the final chapter of the *League of the Iroquois:*

Our Indian relations from the foundation of the Republic to the present moment have been administered with reference to the ultimate advantage of the government itself; while the reclamation of the Indian has been a secondary object, if it ever entered into the calculation to the slightest degree. Millions of money, it is true, have been expended, and some show of justice preserved in their complicated affairs; but in all prominent negotiations the profit has been on the side of the government, and the loss on that of the Indian. In addition to this, instances of sharp-sighted diplomacy, of ungenerous coercion, and of grievous injustice, are to be found in the journal of our Indian transactions—a perpetual stigma upon the escutcheon of our Republic.[1]

Christianity, education, agriculture, and citizenship are his four touchstones which will lead to a solution of the problem:

[1] II, 121. Citations throughout the volume refer to the Lloyd edition of 1904.

There are but two ways of rescueing the Indian from his impending destiny; and these are education and Christianity. If he will receive into his mind the light of knowledge and the spirit of civilization, he will possess not only the means of self-defence, but the power with which to emancipate himself from the thraldom in which he is held.[1]

. . . . When the Iroquois reach such a stable position as agriculturists as to make it safe to divide their lands among the several families of each nation, with the power of alienation, it will give them the stimulus and ambition which separate rights of property are so well calculated to produce. . . . . This would serve to prepare the way for other changes, until finally they would be restored with safety to themselves, not only to the full possession of those rights of property which are common to ourselves, but also to the rights and privileges of citizens of the State.[2]

In an article entitled "Fabrics of the Iroquois," which appeared in July, 1850, he romanticizes on the beneficent effect of agriculture and diffusion of knowledge among the Indians and reveals his glorification of the western expansion movement:

A portion indeed of the Indian family is destined eventually to be reclaimed and raised to citizenship among ourselves. But this can only be accomplished by their adoption of agricultural pursuits and the diffusion of knowledge among them. When this change is affected among them, they will cease to be Indians. A different destiny awaits the residue. At no distant day the war shout of the Red man will fall away into eternal silence, upon the shores of the distant Pacific. Industry will have taken her abode in the seclusions of the forest, the

[1] *Ibid.*, p. 111.   [2] *Ibid.*, p. 119.

church will rise upon the ruins of the council house, the railway pursue the distant trail, the plowshare turn the sod of the hunting ground; and the pursuits of peace having diffused themselves over the whole republic; one universal and continuous hum of industry will rise from ocean to ocean.[1]

Morgan again took up the cudgels for the hounded Indians later in life. With the opening of the railroads and the westward movement of the population the policy of the whites toward the Indians became one of deliberate extermination. General Halleck in 1866 urged that the Apache "be hunted and exterminated"; and General Philip Sheridan, who was commissioned to "pacify" the frontier, epitomized his policy with the slogan, "There are no good Indians but dead Indians." The Sand Creek massacre luridly illustrates the fact that the military forces carried out this policy with a vengeance. Nearly a thousand Colorado volunteers attacked five hundred to six hundred harmless, friendly Cheyenne and Arapahoe Indians, mostly women and children, and brutally slaughtered them. The much heralded raid of General Custer—immortalized by huge lithographs found in every saloon, before the passing of the Eighteenth Amendment—was a similar venture. The behavior of the government in reference to the Sioux had been nothing short of criminal. The Dakotas and Sioux had depended exclusively for subsistence on herds of wild buffalo, which the white settlers and military forces drove from their ranges, depriving the Indians of their food. As early as 1862, the date of the

---

[1] *Stryker's American Register*, July, 1860, p. 343.

first protest of this group, some of the Sioux were in such a state of starvation, not having received their support from the government, that they were forced to subsist on bitter roots and raw corn. In 1868, a disgraceful treaty was offered the Dakotas, which Sitting Bull, their chief, refused. The government then threatened that, unless the Indians moved to their reservation by 1876, they would be treated as hostile Indians, a menace which the Indians disregarded. General Custer was then sent against them, and he and his men met defeat at the hands of these outraged Indians fighting desperately to retain their territory. The press all over the country made of Custer a martyred hero, characterized his defeat as a "ruthless massacre," and instigated a wave of indignation over the country, crying out for revenge. It was against this hysteria for the blood of the Indians that Morgan raised his voice, in an article to the *Nation* entitled, "The Hue and Cry against the Indians":

Who shall blame the the Sioux for defending themselves, their wives and children, when attacked in their own encampment and threatened with destruction? This calamity is simply a chance of war—of a war waged by our government upon these Indians, nothing more and nothing less. For its moral character we must look to the motives which prompted the government in its commencement. . . . .

. . . . Before the summer is over we may expect to hear of the destruction of the great body of these unreasoning and unreasonable Indians, who refuse to treat for the surrender of their lands upon terms they do not approve, and whose extermination may be regarded by some as a merited punishment. The good name of our country cannot bear many wars of this description.

In 1869, Congress had authorized the president to appoint a Board of Indian Commissioners, who, acting with the Secretary of the Interior, should exercise joint control over the expenditures of all appropriations of the Indian Bureau. But there still existed an uncertain division of authority over the Indians between the War and Interior departments, and conflict was rife between these two groups over policy. Many westerners who desired the lands of the Indians preferred to have the Indian country controlled by the army because its barbaric policy of extermination was in accord with their desired treatment of the Indians, whom they characterized as "vipers," and because the army garrisons were a profitable source of revenue for western tradesmen. Those advocating the army policy raised a smoke screen for themselves by exposing the corrupt maladministration of funds of many of the Indian agents. It was this situation that Morgan attacked as he continued in his article:

. . . . A graver objection is the absence of intelligence and judgment in the management of our Indian affairs. It is not so much an objection to the present system as the absence for the last fifty years of anything that can be called a system. The subject has never received the attention it ought to have received because its importance in a moral as well as an economic sense has never been appreciated. It would not have been a mistake fifty years ago, if a department of Indian affairs had been created; it would not be a mistake to create such a department now and place it in the hands of one of the first men of the nation. Something of this kind is needed to extricate our country from the disgrace and reproach which are falling upon it from our failure to perform intelligently our public duty to this unfortunate and declining race. The annual appropriation for Indian objects is now in excess of five million dollars. It is a large sum which under an intelligent system and in the hands of honest men, could have accomplished much good. Indian appropriation bills have never been criticised by the American people. They are willing even anxious that the Government should deal liberally and generously with the Indian race whose gradual destruction seems to be the inevitable result of American progress. But notwithstanding the large expenditures the system of Indian management, if it can be called a system, has been a total failure. At times it has been corrupt. It aims to deal with difficulties as they arise by temporary expedients instead of forecasting their difficulties and preventing their occurrence.[1]

In the next issue of the *Nation*, under the title "The Factory System for Indian Reservations," Morgan urged that it was senseless for the government to feed the Indians in perpetuity under the slogan that it was "cheaper to feed the Indians than to fight them," and maintained that the task was to make them self-supporting. The Dakotas were to be induced to become a pastoral people raising herds of cattle for food to take the place of the departing buffaloes. For other groups, he suggested that the government establish industries, using as a model that of a capitalist enterprise undertaken among the Ojibwa Indians where the Indians made tourist objects yielding the Indians $25,000 and the entrepreneur $15,000 profit. He reveals the implications of his own evolutionary scheme as he wrote about the Indians:

[1] *Nation* (New York), July 20, 1876.

. . . . The Indian tribes must be dealt with as they are—as Indians and not as though they were white men —and with patience and forbearance. They are not only barbarians, but are in a low stage of barbarism, immensely below the plane of civilization. They are incapable of acting in the modes of a civilized race, but they are neither devoid of intelligence nor incapable of appreciating the usual incentives to human action. It will be found possible to stimulate their industry and to lead them gradually into the practice of labor, and with it into an improved plan of life. . . . . The love of property is still a feeble passion in the brains of an Indian; its uses are but little appreciated, and its stimulus but little felt. Their daily food is the principle concern. The men work with untiring diligence in hunting and fishing when game and fish are their principle food, but they have no conception of property as the representative of accumulated subsistence. While they understand the arts of barbarous life, they have but little knowledge of those of civilized life. Any system of management, therefore must be adapted to their mental as well as physical condition if success is expected or desired. . . . .

He added, as the crowning argument purporting to show the success of the model enterprise:

. . . . a marked change for the better had taken place in the social relations of the sexes and in the treatment of the women by the men. They had erected comfortable houses, furnished them with their own furniture and now used tables and sat down together at their meals. . . . .

The inability of the malfunctioning Indian Bureau to carry out treaty stipulations, let alone to initiate new enterprises among the Indians, led Morgan to recom-

mend the creation of a Department of Indian Affairs
with a cabinet officer at its head.

Morgan referred repeatedly to his plan of meeting the
Indian situation, delivering an address on the subject
before the National Academy of Science and also attempting to arouse opinion by letters to public men.
Among those to whom he wrote was Benjamin Albord,
then paymaster general. Upon receipt of Morgan's letter, Albord responded:

. . . . After getting your letter I called on President
Hayes and mentioned your name, your views and your
labors. He had seen some of your writings and I think
that if you will call on him you will find him prepared to
talk to you. . . . .[1]

Morgan then addressed the following communication
to President Hayes:

As a citizen I feel at liberty to address you on a public
question, which may deserve your official attention as
President of the United States.

The time has arrived as it seems to me, when, to begin
with conclusions, Congress should create a "Department
of Indian Affairs," with a cabinet officer at its head,
with a view to the institution of a new system of management of the affairs of our Indian tribes. The point of
my suggestion is that these tribes cannot be successfully
managed by a commission under the Secretary of the
Interior. We have a right to assume that our past experience has demonstrated this proposition. It is certain that a new Department of the government, under a
competent head can do it. But such a measure is the
best and last chance which the American people can
offer for the successful management of our Indian
Affairs.

[1] Dated Capon Springs, Virginia, July 31, 1877.

The need of some movement, radical in character and supported and clothed with sufficient power, is evident to all. The country is ready for such a movement, and, as I believe, would give to it a cordial welcome.

It rests with you to decide upon the advisability of such a Department, and if your conclusion is affirmative, to inaugurate the measure by recommending it to Congress. I hope exceedingly that you will do this at the approaching session, with an indication of the scheme of a law giving adequate powers in the premises.

Although there are but 400,000 Indians in the United States an insignificant number of people in the aggregate they are scattered over all the Territories, where they meet our people at numerous points: and they are also found in places in several of the States. They and their posterity will live in our midst for centuries to come, because Indian arts for the maintenance of life are far more persistent and effective than we are disposed to credit.

The Indian tribes hold a more important position in their relations to us than their numbers would imply. It is for the reason that they form no part of our social and political system. They are without the pale of our political society and are not a constituent portion of our people. But as the aborigines of the country and its ancient proprietors they stand to us in a special relation, a relation in some respects awful to contemplate. We are responsible for them before mankind.

Two instrumentalities may be named which have at least the promise of good. One is the establishment of a factory system for such tribes as have long been accustomed to settled life on reservations. It would stimulate and reward their industry which is never wanting among their women. The second is a pastoral system for the Indians of the plains, which is the most important of the two because it would reach those tribes where disturbances are constantly arising.

We have overlooked the fact that the principal Indian

tribes have passed, by natural development, out of the condition of savages into that of barbarians. In relative progress they are now precisely where our own barbarous ancestors were when by the domestication of animals, they passed from a lower into a higher condition of barbarism, through still two ethnical periods below civilization. Their great progress commenced when they gained through flocks and herds of domestic animals a permanent milk and meat subsistence. We wonder that our Indians cannot civilize; but how could they any more than our remote ancestors, jump ethnical periods. They have the brains and skulls of barbarians, and must grow towards civilization, as all mankind have done who attained to civilization by a progressive experience.

The next condition into which the Indian tribes would naturally advance is the pastoral. They have learned unassisted to raise horses in herds. They can be taught to raise domestic cattle in herds. Here the government should help them by furnishing herds of cattle and by sending herdsmen to take care of them until they can be made to see that the natural increase will afford them an abundant meat and milk subsistence. This will solve the problem and recast their destiny. In time they will raise cattle in millions on the plains, as buffaloes have raised themselves in millions on the same plains. The Indian tribes would thus be contented prosperous and happy and make a proper use of regions of no present use or value to our people.

As an economic question, we have a direct interest in this matter ourselves. If innumerable herds of domestic animals are created on the vast central prairies, they would become a source of meat supply for the entire country east of the Mississippi. It would cost the government but a small part of the sum annually expended upon the Indians to establish this great work, with every appearance that it would solve the Indian problem by raising the Indian tribes of the plains into a condition of prosperity, not to say of health, and by making them in the place of a plague an ultimate source of benefit to the country by contributing to its prosperity.

I need not take your time to amplify these propositions. The present system has failed completely. It is discreditable to the country. Any new movement having a fair promise of success will be received with favor because the entire country would be glad to see the Indian affairs in a more reputable condition.[1]

President Hayes's message to Congress that year gave evidence of Morgan's influence, although not including his recommendation of creating a new department. After blandly declaring, "Many if not most of our Indian wars have their origin in broken promises and acts of injustice on our part . . . .," he stated:

. . . . Especial care is recommended to provide for Indians settled on their reservations cattle and agricultural implements, to aid them in whatever efforts they make to support themselves, and by the establishment and maintenance of schools to bring them under the control of civilized influences.[2]

Morgan again reiterated his plea for a Department of Indian Affairs in the *Nation* of November 28, 1878. Among the responses which the letter provoked were those of Professor F. W. Putnam, of Harvard, and of the editor of the *Nation*, Wendell Phillips Garrison. Professor Putnam promised possible assistance:

[1] Dated Rochester, New York, August 6, 1877.

[2] "First Annual Message of Rutherford B. Hayes to Senate and House of Representatives, December 3, 1877," *Messages and Papers of the Presidents*, X, 4427.

I have just read your letter in the *Nation*. Can't some action be taken to bring about the state of Indian management you propose? Have you any plan of action? I believe so thoroughly that some such plan as you propose is the only hope for the Indians that I shall be glad to do all I can in working with you to bring it about, and it seems to me with your influence and world wide reputation as writer on Indians and their proper management in order to aid them in their march to civilization, that you could bring about the happy result you have proposed as possible.[1]

Garrison was emphatic in his sympathy with the project:

The only objection I have to your *Indian letter* is that it cuts from under me the basis of an article I had in mind on the same subject. That objection I need hardly add is so far from being fatal that I am conscious of being grateful to you for anticipating me and for saying well what I should have said badly even if with good intent. It is high time the country were made aware that the army cannot originate an Indian policy, and that its execution of "no-policy" would never solve the problem.[2]

XV

Morgan won for himself many devoted friends, among whom were William Cullen Bryant, Joseph Henry, Andrew D. White, Henry A. Ward, Eben Norton Horsford, and other members of the Harvard faculty, in addition to his ethnological, political, and business associates, his neighbors, and the clergymen and missionaries whom he delighted to entertain. He was founder of the Anthro-

[1] Dated Cambridge, Massachusetts, November 30, 1878.
[2] Dated New York, November 25, 1878.

pological Section of the American Association for the Advancement of Science and was president of the Association in 1880. An enthusiastic "joiner," he belonged to many social and scientific societies and initiated clubs from his youth until his final years. Among these was "The Club," patterned after a similar organization to which Albert Gallatin had belonged. Before this group, composed of professional men and a few business men, Morgan tried out his ideas prior to putting them in final form. To the members of "The Club" he always felt grateful for assisting him in the task he found most difficult, that of clarifying his hypotheses after he had accumulated his data. For Morgan, though interested in learning, was not erudite. He was capable of persistent compilation of factual data and of bold, if hazardous, generalizations, as the analysis of his work will reveal.

CHAPTER II

THE LEAGUE OF THE IROQUOIS

I

The addresses which Morgan delivered to the members of the "New Confederacy of the Iroquois," in their combined form in the *League of the Ho de no sau nee or Iroquois*, make excellent ethnological material when measured by the standards of the period in which they were written. The book has the glaring deficiencies and inadequacies of a pioneer work. But compared to Henry R. Schoolcraft's contemporary study, *Notes of the Iroquois*, it represents a marked advance in the technique of recording the customs and social organization of primitive peoples. Morgan was here primarily a sympathetic amateur with a tendency to romanticize and sentimentalize about a departing people, but he manifests his keen ability to observe and record ethnological data. The book contains many concepts upon which Morgan later developed.

After a dedication to Ely S. Parker,[1] whom he acknowledges as a collaborator, and a Preface stating the

---

[1] Parker, whose Indian name was at this time *Ha sa no an da*, "Coming to the Front," and who later received the name *Do ne ho ga wa*, as eighth Sachem of the Seneca tribe, became a friend of Ulysses S. Grant when he was employed as a government engineer in Galena, Illinois. Later, he was made a member of Grant's staff and was his chief secretary. In 1869–71 he was Commissioner of Indian Affairs under General Grant. (*League of the Iroquois*, II, 179–81.)

purpose of the book epitomized by the sentence, "The time has come in which it is befitting to cast away all ancient antipathies, all inherited opinions; and having taken a nearer view of their [the Iroquois's] social life, conditions and wants, to study anew our duty concerning them," the book opens with a brief historical and geographical setting to the League. W. M. Beauchamp, a later historian of the Iroquois, though commending highly other parts of the *League of the Iroquois*, is severely critical of these chapters:

. . . . When we go back of the present century, there is very little in it that will stand the test of even moderate criticism. His map of the Iroquois country is that of modern days not of the old villages and trails, of which he knew next to nothing. He abandoned the old traditions long on record for the extravagant statements of Cusick, the Tuscarora historian.[1]

Of the French writers on this subject, Morgan knew only "the not always reliable Charlevoix and the always unreliable La Hontan."[2] Morgan later engaged in an extended correspondence over the aboriginal geography of the region with John S. Clark and O. W. Marshall, and in his other writings modified his opinions.

Morgan's discussion of the League and the clan system implied that they were established by a conscious act of legislation; and this view was immediately challenged by Francis Parkman in his review of the book.[3] Subsequent investigations have also disproved Morgan's

[1] *American Antiquarian*, IX, 343–50.

[2] *League of the Iroquois*, II, 150.

[3] *Christian Examiner*, May, 1861. Cf. his *Conspiracy of Pontiac*, I, 12.

opinion, also held by Horatio Hale, the linguist, author of *Myths of the Iroquois*, that the League was founded a century and one-half before the coming of the Dutch, Hewitt establishing the date as about 1570. Morgan's assertions about the relationship of the Iroquois to other tribes were based on the insufficient data at his disposal and have no value.

It is in his analysis of the structure of the League that Morgan was at his best, for it was for the purpose of modeling his secret society after the pattern of the League that his investigations were initiated. In the beginning of the discussion, Morgan gives evidence of having abstracted the League from its background without understanding the basic economic life of the people. In spite of the fact that the Iroquois lived largely by agriculture, he wrote:

The passion of the red man for the hunter life has proved to be a principle too deeply inwrought to be controlled by efforts of legislation. His government, if one was sought to be established, must have conformed to this irresistible tendency of his mind, this inborn sentiment; otherwise it would have been disregarded. The effect of this powerful principle has been to enchain the tribes of North America to their primitive state. . . . . We have here the true reason why the red race has never risen, nor can rise above its present level.[1]

He struck the false note in this book that was to pervade all his writings when he wrote, "Their [the Iroquois'] institutions contain the sum and substance of those of the whole Indian family."[2] But Morgan's actual description of the organization of the structure of the

[1] *League of the Iroquois*, I, 53–54.   [2] *Ibid.*, p. 52.

League has become a classic, although it has required some revision in fact and in nomenclature by the findings of later studies.

Morgan, in portraying the interrelationship of the clans [called "tribes" in this book], noted the method of indicating relationship among the Iroquois, the discussion of which kinship system was to make him famous. Considering his later insistence of the universality of this kinship system, it is interesting to note the following comment:

The Iroquois claim to have originated the idea of a division of the people into tribes, as a means of creating new relationships by which to bind the people more firmly together. . . . . The fact that this division of the people of the same nation into tribes does not prevail generally among our Indian races, favors the assertion of the Iroquois.[1]

In his discussion of the government of the Iroquois he expatiates on the political classifications of Aristotle and Montesquieu, and violates the principle which he later stressed and for which American ethnology owes him its greatest debt, that a primitive people should be interpreted in terms of its own culture and not in terms of that of the investigator. Of this discussion Herbert M. Lloyd, who later edited this book, wrote: "It is Morgan's own work, as much as any man's, that has made the fine philosophy of the Sixth Chapter of Book I, concerning the origin and development of governments, as much an antique curiosity as a crossbow or a horse-car."[2] In the light of his later teachings, the following discussion is peculiarly incongruous:

[1] *Ibid.*, p. 87.   [2] *Ibid.*, II, 150.

The order of their origination suggests an important general principle; that there is a regular progression of political institutions from the monarchical which are the earliest in time, on to the democratical, which are the last, the noblest and the most intellectual. . . . . An unlimited monarchy, or "the rule of a single individual according to his will," is the form of government natural to a people when in an uncivilized state, or when just emerging from barbarism. In the progress of time, by the growth and expansion of civil liberty the monarchy becomes liberalized or limited and a few steps forward introduce universal democracy. Hence it is noticeable in the rise of all races, and in the formation of all states, that the idea of chief and follower, or sovereign and people, is of spontaneous suggestion. This notion may be regarded as inherent to society in its primitive state.[1]

A clue to the implication of Morgan's emphasis on the influence of property organization on other aspects of social organization is given here:

At this point the singular trait in the character of the red man suggests itself, that he never felt the "power of gain." The *auri sacra fames* of Virgil, the *studium lucri* of Horace, never penetrated his nature. This great passion of the civilized man, in its use and abuse, its blessing and its curse, never aroused the Indian mind. It was doubtless the great reason of his continuance in the hunter state; for the desire of gain is one of the earliest manifestations of progressive mind, and one of the most powerful passions of which the mind is susceptible. It clears the forest, rears the city, builds the merchantman, in a word, it has civilized our race.[2]

[1] *Ibid.*, I, 122.

[2] *Ibid.*, p. 131. In the original article an additional phrase followed the second sentence: "To him alike the gold and brass, the luxuries and vanities of life."

Most ethnologists before the appearance of Tylor's disquisition on primitive religion assumed that primitive man had no religion. Morgan did not fall into this error; but his discussion of the religion of the Iroquois is unsatisfactory as ethnologic material, for, instead of giving a clear picture of Iroquois ceremonies and beliefs, he interpreted them in terms of Greek and Christian religious concepts. Such characteristic interpretations result as:

That the Indian without the aid of revelation, should have arrived at a fixed belief in the existence of one Supreme Being, has ever been a matter of surprise and admiration. In the existence of the Great Spirit, an invisible but ever-present Deity, the universal red race believed. His personal existence became a first principle, an intuitive belief, which neither the lapse of centuries could efface, nor inventions of man could corrupt. By the diffusion of this great truth, if the Indian did not escape the spell of superstition, which resulted from his imperfect knowledge of the Deity, and his ignorance of natural phenomena; yet he was saved from the deepest of all barbarisms, an idolatrous worship. . . . . The ennobling and exalting views of the Deity which are now held by enlightened and Christian nations would not be expected among a people excluded from the light of revelation. . . . . Such is the power of truth over the human mind, and the harmony of all truth, that the Indian, without the power of logic, reached some of the most important conclusions of philosophy, and drew down from heaven some of the highest truths of revelation.[1]

His descriptions of the maple-planting, berry, green-corn, harvest, and white-dog festivals are valuable al-

[1] *Ibid.*, pp. 146–47.

though vitiated by pious Christian asides and moralizings. His inclusion of the verbatim speech of *Dɑ at ga dose* on the new religion of *Ga ne o di yo* is his closest approach to the technique of modern ethnology.

It is in Morgan's analysis of the implements and fabrics of the Seneca that he was at his best. These chapters were originally written as reports for the New York State Museum and dispense with the sententious oratory, sophomoric eloquence, and sentimental rhapsodizing that permeates those delivered as addresses before the "New Confederacy." His description of these objects and his accompanying illustrations are reliable and accurate, revealing a rare gift of discriminating observation and facility in description. Students of the Iroquois have declared his treatment of this phase of the Seneca culture priceless, although they point out correctly that Morgan erred in thinking that, by describing the Seneca implements and fabrics, he was portraying those of all the Iroquois. In his exposition, Morgan made little attempt to distinguish between original objects and patterns and those which were Indian adaptations of European patterns.

Morgan includes a brief chapter on the language of the Iroquois, which is unsatisfactory in method and content even as compared with the treatment of Indian languages by his contemporaries. His description of the houses, marriage, and marriage customs is very cursory, considering his later intense interest in these subjects; and crime among the Iroquois is analyzed in terms of European codes and standards.

The great lack of the *League of the Iroquois* is its

absence of adequate treatment of the economic life of the people. Their hunting customs and regulations are given very desultory treatment, and their agricultural life next to none. Had Morgan been more aware of this fundamental aspect of Iroquois life, his treatment of their political, religious, and social life would have received different emphasis. But Morgan had his eyes on the Confederacy and its machinery as a model for his "New Confederacy." All else is incidental material gathered to give some reality to the purpose of the secret society established to perpetuate a knowledge of Indian custom and lore. Dramatic, exotic material which would appeal to the members of the secret society assembled around the council fire was stressed.

In his desire to overcome the great antagonism to the Indians among the whites, Morgan romanticizes over and extols the Indian and his culture, but he never casts off the attitude of a Christian white man observing an "inferior" culture. His treatment of the material, except that dealing with fabrics and implements, is that of a humanitarian pleading the cause of an outraged people, not alone that of an ethnologist studying their culture to acquire scientific data. But the book, though supplemented and revised by later studies, has remained the classic treatment of the Iroquois peoples. It has been and still is quoted extensively in all parts of the world by ethnologists and historians.

II

It was also during the period of his affiliation with the "New Confederacy of the Iroquois" that Morgan edited anonymously J. E. Seaver's *Narrative of the Life of Mary Jemison: Deh he wa mis*, appending notes derived from the *League of the Iroquois*.[1] The Introductory Note portrays his motivation in editing and publishing the volume, and throws further light on his intellectual orientation at that time:

. . . . it is hoped that a perusal of the book may excite a greater detestation of the horrors of war, and of a spirit of revenge, and a clearer view of the necessity of an adoption of the gospel of Christ to render either nations or individuals truly happy, as well as give a correct delineation of Indian manners and customs.[2]

In the Preface to this book Morgan spoke of intermarriage between Indians and whites as an "unnatural alliance." Later he was very indecisive on this point. In a communication to Daniel Wilson of Toronto, author of *Prehistoric Man*, he stated:

I have visited all the emigrant nations in Kansas and Nebraska with two or three exceptions. I saw instances among the Shawnees and Delawares, and the Wyandots in Kansas where white men who had married half-breed Indian women were living genteely among them, and had slaves to cultivate their land; and also instances where half-breed Indians had married white wives and were living in good style. . . . . When the Indian acquires property, and with it education, and becomes permanently settled, then honorable marriage will commence, and with it a transfer of the posterity to our ranks. I hope to see that day arrive; for I think we can

[1] The book went into many editions, the Putnam edition of 1910 containing a formal acknowledgment of the authorship of the notes and Preface. Morgan's Preface is dated July, 1847.

[2] *Narrative of the Life of Mary Jemison*, p. vii.

absorb a large portion of this Indian blood, with an increase of physical strength and no intellectual detriment. . . . .[1]

In his *Systems of Consanguinity*, Morgan's attitude again varies, and he ventures a naïve explanation for the possible unsatisfactory nature of miscegenation between the two races:

. . . . The Indian and European are at opposite poles in their physiological conditions. In the former there is very little animal passion, while with the latter it is superabundant. A pure-blooded Indian has very little animal passion, but in the half-blood it is sensibly augmented; and when the second generation is reached with a cross giving three-fourths white blood, it becomes excessive and tends to indiscriminate licentiousness. If this be true in fact, it is a potent adverse element leading to demoralization and decay, which it will be extremely difficult to overmaster and finally escape. In this native state, the Indian is below the passion of love. It is entirely unknown among them, with the exception, to a limited extent, of the Village Indians. This fact is sufficiently proved by the universal prevalence of the custom of disposing of the females in marriage without their knowledge or participation in the arrangement. The effects produced by intermixture of European and Indian blood, although a delicate subject, is one of scientific interest. The facts above stated I obtained from traders and trappers on the Upper Missouri, who have spent their lives in the Indian country, and understand Indian life in all its relations. When at the Red River Settlement in 1861, I made this a subject of further inquiry, the results of which tended to confirm the above statements. Whether this abnormal or disturbed state of the

[1] Dated April 24, 1861. Cf. Daniel Wilson, *Prehistoric Man*, pp. 541–43, 557.

animal passions will finally subside into a proper equilibrium, is one of the questions involved. There was much
in the thrift, industry, and intelligence displayed at the
Settlement to encourage the hope and the expectation of
an ultimately successful solution of the problem. Among
the pure Orkney men, as well as half-bloods, there were
many excellent and solid men who would command respect and attain success in any community; and under
such influences the probabilities of success are greatly
strengthened. As far as my personal observation has extended among the American Indian nations, the half-
blood is inferior, both physically and mentally, to the
pure Indian; but the second cross, giving three-quarters
Indian, is an advance upon the native; and giving three-
fourths white is a still greater advance, approximating to
equality with the white ancestor. With the white carried
still further, full equality is reached, tending to show
that Indian blood can be taken up without physical or
intellectual detriment.[1]

Morgan's failure to distinguish between biological and
cultural phenomena, which make this discussion so
ludicrous, is consistently revealed in other aspects of
his work.

[1] *Systems of Consanguinity*, pp. 206–7.

CHAPTER III

SYSTEMS OF CONSANGUINITY

I

When Morgan had first noted the features of the Iroquois system of consanguinity in 1846 among the Senecas, he considered it their invention; and ten years later, when he delivered a paper entitled the "Laws of Descent of the Iroquois" at the Montreal meeting of the American Association for the Advancement of Science,[1] he still had no evidence that the system extended beyond the Iroquois.

In the summer of 1858, however, he discovered substantially the same system among the Ojibwa in Wisconsin. He wrote of this discovery in his journal:

From this time I began to be sensible to the important uses which such a primary institution as this must have in its bearing upon the question of the genetic connection of the American Indian nation, not only, but also on the still more important question of their Asiatic origin.[2]

Upon his return to Rochester, he immediately consulted Rigg's lexicon of the Dakota language; and finding features of the system also among this group, he set about at once to prepare a questionnaire to secure data elsewhere.

[1] *Proceedings of the Eleventh Meeting of the American Association for the Advancement of Science*, August, 1856, Sec. 2, pp. 132–48.

[2] Dated October 19, 1859.

As early as December, 1858, Morgan demonstrated in a circular letter the significance which he had attached to his discovery and his objective in making an extended investigation:

Ethnological researches have failed to demonstrate the unity of the race. They have grouped under a few generic families the races of Europe, Asia and America, but beyond this they fail to give us light. Our interest in the inquiry is by no means satisfied.

It has occurred to me after some examination that we may yet find some clue by which to trace our Indian races with certainty into Northern Asia by means of their institutions, some of which in the nature of things are more permanent than language, which not only changes its vocabulary, but advances its grammatical structure by development.

Again in the letter prefaced to the eight-page schedule questionnaire which he sent to missionaries and to Indian agents in January, 1859, he stated his hypotheses:

It has occurred to me, after careful examination of the system of consanguinity and descent of the Iroquois, that we may yet be able, by means of it to solve the question whether our Indian races are of Asiatic origin. Language changes its vocabulary not only, but also modifies its grammatical structure in the progress of ages; thus eluding the inquiries which philologists have pressed it to answer; but a system of consanguinity once matured and brought into working operation, is in the nature of things, more unchangeable than language; not in the names employed as a vocabulary of relationship but in the ideas which underlie the system itself. The Indo-European nations have one system identical in its principal features, with an antiquity of thirty-five centuries, as a fact of actual record. That of the Iroquois is originally clearly defined, and the reverse of the former. It is, at least to be presumed that it has an antiquity coeval. That of the Chippewas is the same as the Iroquois with slight modifications; thus establishing the fact of its existence in two of the principal generic stocks. Besides this there are traces of the same system among the Aztecs, Mohaves, Creeks, Dakotas, Winnebagoes and other races, all tending to show that the system has been, and now is universal upon this continent. Should this last fact be established, the antiquity of the system, as coeval with the Indian race upon the continent, will also become established. Upon the basis of these two facts, and assuming that these races are of Asiatic origin we may predict the existence of the same system in Asia, at the present moment, among the descendants of their common ancestors, if any remain.

The tribal organization and the system of relationship, lie at the foundation of Indian society. They represent and express ideas as old as the race itself—ideas as unchangeable as ancient and freighted with testimony of the highest ethnological value. Upon precisely such ideas as these which have been deposited in the family life of a race we can, if by any instrumentality, ascend through the generations up to the fountain of descent, not only; but retrace as well, the footsteps of migrations long since buried under the shadows of departed ages. Along the pathway of these successive generations— marked with epochs of migration from age to age—every divergence of family from the parent stock would carry with it the same ideas spreading them upon the track of each new migration—perchance into the most distant parts of the earth. It is barely possible, there is some chance, enough to encourage the research, that with a thread as delicate, almost invisible as this, we may yet ascend quite near to the times and places of these several divergencies, and reassociate races and nations, whose origin and ancient connection have long since passed from the knowledge of men.

The returns from these questionnaires were at first very meager, though not entirely a failure, due to the receipt of the complete system of the Minnesota Dakotas worked out by S. R. Riggs, and that of a few other partially complete schedules. Excited at his discovery and impatient and eager to test out his generalization of the universality of the system in North America, Morgan determined to pursue his investigations in person. In May and June, 1859, he made an expedition through Kansas and Nebraska, gathering data on kinship systems. He delivered a paper at the Springfield meeting of the American Association for the Advancement of Science in August of that year, entitled "The Indian Modes of Bestowing and Changing Names," based on his investigations. In it he contends that the same social organization and customs are prevalent among all the Indian groups and that this fact has "an important bearing upon the question of a common origin of the race."

It was after the delivery of this paper that Morgan learned that the unilateral system of tracing kinship extended beyond the American continent, a discovery which overwhelmed him with its importance. He thus records it in the original entry of his journal:

I come now to the most interesting and extraordinary event in the history of this inquiry: a discovery which attests the value of this new instrument in ethnological research, and which also affords some promise of its great future usefulness. Having ascertained that Dr.

Henry W. Scudder of the Arcot Mission in Southern India was in this country, I enclosed a schedule and letter to him and requested him to furnish me the Tamil system of relationship. After some correspondence, I received a final answer containing the principal features of the Tamilian system of consanguinity in the month of August last and shortly after my return from Springfield. My astonishment was greater than I could express to learn that the Tamil system and the American Indian system were substantially identical; and that too, in the most special and intricate features which characterise the two systems. On the 15th day of August last I replied to Dr. Scudder at length laying the two systems side by side and expressing the belief that we had now been able to put our hands upon decisive evidence of the Asiatic origin of the American Indian Race.

Shortly after this I visited Dr. Scudder at Milton Ulster Co. N. Y. and obtained both a Tamil and Telugu schedule as far forth as he was able to furnish that without consulting a native. He informed me that he had had occasion to verify with a qualified native scholar, the several relationships which he gave me and that I might rely upon their entire accuracy. The systems of the Tamil and Telugu races who number about twenty-four millions of people are substantially identical.[1]

McIlvaine corroborates Morgan's testimony as to the surprise his discovery occasioned and the zest with which Morgan undertook his inquiry:

During this period he lived and worked often in a state of great mental excitement and the answers he received as they came in sometimes nearly overpowered him. I well remember one occasion when he came into my study saying "I shall find it, I shall find it among the Tamil people and Dravidian tribes of Southern

[1] Dated October 19, 1859.

India." At this time I had no expectation of any such result and I said to him, "My friend, you have enough to do in working out your discovery in connection with the tribes of the American continent, let the peoples of the old world go." He replied "I cannot do it—I cannot do it, I must go on, for I am sure I shall find it all there." Some months afterward, he came in again, his face all aglow with excitement, the Tamil schedule in his hands, the answers to his questions just what he had predicted, and throwing it on my table, he exclaimed "There! what did I tell you!"[1]

At the Springfield meeting, Professor Joseph Henry, of the Smithsonian Institution, had become interested in Morgan's inquiry. He secured the indorsement of General Lewis Cass, then Secretary of State, and gave Morgan the mailing facilities of the Smithsonian Institution to send out hundreds of letters and schedules to United States agents in all parts of the world. The reprint of the circular letter made in October, 1859, was essentially the same as the earlier letter, but the revised wording clarifies his objectives:

The universal prevalence among the North American Indians, of a system of consanguinity and relationship so exceedingly complex was sufficiently remarkable to suggest some questions as to what might be its ethnological value. Its permanency was sufficiently illustrated by its universal prevalence through a long period of time, in which every word of some of the languages had undergone such changes as to be wholly unintelligible to the people of other languages in which the system itself had undergone no material modification. Consequently it seemed to indicate the unity of origin of all

[1] Eulogy reprinted in Lloyd's edition of *League of the Iroquois*, II, 169 *et seq.*

these Indian nations, which though probable before, was not so well established as to leave undesirable the further evidence to be derived from this source. The ancientness upon this continent of the Red race, assuming its original unity, was rendered manifest by the number of ages which would be required for an original language to fall into several languages so entirely changed in their vocabularies as to lose all internal evidence, from this source, of their original connection; and for these in turn to fall into the multitudinous dialects in which they are now spoken. This permanency and this universality of the system, therefore, could scarcely be understood, in any other way than by the assumption that this system itself was as old as the Indian race on this continent. If, then, the Red race was of Asiatic origin, it became very probable that they brought it with them from Asia, and left it behind them in the stock from which they separated.

He then tells of his discovery of the similarities in the Tamil and Telugu schedules with those of the Iroquois and Dakota, and continues:

Can these coincidences be accidental? While this is not the proper place to discuss either the extent or the conclusiveness of the evidence afforded of the Asiatic origin of the American Indian race, yet it is not too much to say, that the remarkable similarity of their systems of consanguinity, in many special features, furnishes no slight indication that further research will draw forth such additional evidence as may lead to a final solution of this problem.

Should this fact become thus established, we cannot fail to perceive the important bearing which a comparison of the several systems of consanguinity and relationship of the human race will have upon the remaining question of their common origin. Language which has been the great instrument of this inquiry, changes its vocabulary not only, but also modifies its grammatical structure in the progress of ages, thus losing the certainty of its indications, with each new foothold gained in the past. But the ideas deposited in a system of consanguinity, and standing to each other in such fixed relations as to create a system, are mostly independent of all changes in language, and of lapse of time, and depend for their vitality in the human mind, upon their prime necessity and approved usefulness. The system of the Indo-European nations has stood without essential change for upwards of thirty centuries in the lexicons of the Latin, Greek and Sanscrit languages. That of the Tamil and Telugu has an antiquity equally great, having survived the Brahminical conquest, the substitution of a new religion, and the imposition upon them of the law of caste; while that of the American Indians bears internal evidence of the same great age and permanency. . . . . It is not impossible that we may, at no distant day, be able to re-ascend the several lines of outflow of the generations and reach and identify that parent stock, from which we believe we are all alike descended.

The first response to his inquiry which Morgan records in his diary is that from Townsend Harris, minister resident at Yedo, Japan, stating that it was impossible to furnish the data for want of competent interpreters. Morgan comments, "This book will no doubt contain a record of a large number of similar failures." It did. The response to the hundreds of inquiries sent out was very sparse, and letter after letter gave excuses and incomplete data. Material assembled very slowly, and he was obliged to supplement his findings by further field trips. In 1860 he went again to Kansas and Nebraska, extending his journey far up the Missouri River. In 1861 he made a trip to the Hudson Bay territory and Lake Winnipeg, and in 1862 to Fort Benton and the Rocky Mountains.

Comment on the inquiry while it was in process will indicate the reaction of the contemporary American ethnologists to his study. Henry R. Schoolcraft encouraged him:

You have by the Indian consanguinities found a new element in comparing the old occidental and oriental mind. Language has been our principal religious heritage. I have aimed to compare ancient mind with mind by theology and religious ideas. The light you are likely to get promises to be very important and very interesting, at least if you push the matter as you intend.[1]

Dr. L. V. Hayden and George Gibbs supplied him with carefully filled-out schedules, but dissented on his interpretations. Hayden wrote:

That you will succeed in producing a most important work as a contribution to Ethnology, I now consider a settled fact, but still I do not think that you will by it prove the logical unity of the Human race. . . . .[2]

And again:

. . . . but the conclusion which you have described to draw from your labors I have always considered an illogical one.[3]

Gibbs averred:

To tell the truth I am not a believer in the Asiatic origin of the Indians. I think Morton and Agassiz right

[1] Dated Washington, D.C., November 1, 1859.
[2] Dated Deer Creek, Nebraska, December 18, 1859.
[3] Dated June 21, 1860.

in pronouncing them, like the buffalo and grizzly bear, indigenous, and I suspect the buffalo country was mother of nations on this continent as the north of Europe was on the old, though in a really primitive sense.[1]

By November, 1861, Morgan had obtained 48 complete schedules and had begun to formulate his material in some schematic manner. On November 18 of that year he wrote to Lord Stanley, outlining his project:

. . . . My aim is 1. to attempt a new classification of the Indian nations of North America upon the basis of their Systems of Consanguinity and to show through evidence from this source their unity of origin. 2. To show the lines of the original migrations on this continent which their system unfolds in a remarkable manner. 3. To show, if possible their Asiatic origin, by a comparison of their system with those of Asiatic nations.

His problem then became one of interpretation of the material, and here he manifested very pronouncedly his inadequate equipment to deal with the complicated and intricate implications of his work. For five years, during which time schedules came in until he had data on 139 groups, he struggled with the material and then submitted his results to the Smithsonian Institution for publication in January, 1866. The manuscript met opposition, as is indicated by the Prefatory Note to the volume by Dr. Henry:

The present memoir was first referred to a commission consisting of Professor J. H. McIlvaine and Professor William Henry Green of Princeton, New Jersey, who recommended its publication, but advised certain

[1] Dated Northwestern Boundary Survey, March 20, 1859.

changes in the method of presenting the subject. After these modifications had been made, it was submitted to the American Oriental Society, and was by it referred to a special committee, consisting of Messrs. Hadley, Trumbull and Whitney, who after having critically examined the memoir, reported that it contained a series of highly interesting facts which they believed the students of philology and ethnology, though they might not accept all the conclusions of the author, would welcome as valuable contributions to science.[1]

It was finally accepted for publication in January, 1868. Impatient at the delay in publishing the manuscript after its acceptance and fearing that someone else would claim priority of discovery, Morgan presented the conclusions of his study before the Academy of Arts and Sciences in 1868, under the title of "A Conjectural Solution of the Origin of the Classificatory System of Relationship." The volume was finally brought out as one of the Smithsonian "Contributions to Knowledge," under the title *Systems of Consanguinity and Affinity of the Human Family* in June, 1870.

II

Contemporary reactions to *Systems of Consanguinity* in letters which Morgan received from American and European scientists and in reviews will be quoted at some length in view of the erroneous belief in some quarters that Morgan did not receive recognition during his lifetime. Francis Parkman wrote him from Harvard:

I am particularly glad to have the record of your very interesting and curious research in a permanent form.

[1] *Systems of Consanguinity*, p. iii.

If all our savants pushed their inquiries with the same admirable perseverance, vigor and spirit of truth, many dark questions would be solved and our national character for superficiality be, like slavery, a thing of the past.[1]

Oliver Wendell Holmes, Jr., acknowledging the receipt of the volume, commented:

I thank you most sincerely for it and receive it with all the pride which an American has a right to feel in a countryman who has presented such a mass of original facts in the light of general principles which he is one of the first to explain.[2]

Later he reciprocated with two of his studies and wrote:

Will you be kind enough to receive as a kind of feudal acknowledgement—like a pair of gloves or a hawk—not as a worthy animal return—a couple of articles entitled "Primitive Notions in Modern Law. . . . ."[3]

Horatio Hale, while laudatory, reserved judgment:

. . . . The conclusions you have drawn from them [the systems of relationship] in relation to the early condition and progress of various races, appear to me most important. There are, however, some suggestions in regard to them, growing mainly out of the Hawaiian series of relationships, which have occurred to me and I may hereafter take the liberty of submitting them to you.[4]

Professor T. N. Roberts was especially effusive:

I am delighted with the storehouse of facts and ethnographical information with which the work is replete. It will afford a foundation for broad induction and gen-

[1] Dated Boston, November 21, 1868.
[2] Dated Boston, October 15, 1873.
[3] Dated Boston, August 9, 1877.
[4] Dated Clinton, Ontario, November 29, 1869.

eralization in the Science of Sociology. I had no conception that there was a work of such comprehensive reach upon this inaccessible and difficult subject. It ought to be published in such liberal manner that it could be more in reach of the public. I shall endeavor to so use it that it will I hope be of some service in the matter of education. Our Chairs of History in most American colleges have a very narrow range. Ethnography and the broader inductions of a real Social Science, are so cognate—are in fact so fundamental in their relation to History that it is a matter of surprise that any competent knowledge can be expected of it without some knowledge, at least, of these related branches. As for the study of Law, as it is pursued in this country and the grosser practice of legislation, it would never be allowed for a moment if the public had an adequate conception of the bearing of the cognate sciences upon the structure and foundations of society.[1]

It was in England that this work of Morgan's received most attention and provoked most discussion. Charles Darwin, in friendly letters, acknowledged the receipt of the book:

I am much obliged for your extremely kind letter and your present of the concluding chapter which I am sure I shall read with the greatest interest. . . . .

I fully agree with your remarks as to the extreme importance of studying the habits and institutions, if they can be so called, of savages. I have had lately to attend a little to the subject, as I have sent a MS. to the printer for a work on the "Descent of Man," but I have chiefly to treat of veritably primeval times before man was fully man. With much respect for your admirable investigations, believe me, ...[2]

[1] Dated Columbia, South Carolina, September 24, 1877.

[2] Dated Down, Beckenham, Kent, August 11, 1871.

I have received this morning your grand work on Consanguinity, etc. and I am astonished at the labor which it must have cost you.

I am greatly indebted to this proof of your kind feelings toward me and I remain yours very sincerely.[1]

In view of the great influence of Herbert Spencer on popular views of the evolution of the family, his letter to Morgan is very significant:

I am indebted to you for the present of your great work on *Systems of Consanguinity and Affinity* which lately reached me. Hitherto I have had but time to glance through it and to be impressed with the value of its immense mass of materials collected and arranged with so much labor.

I thank you for it in more than the mere formal way that is common in the acknowledgment of presentation copies: for it comes to me at a time when I am making elaborate preparations personally and by deputy for the scientific treatment of Sociology and its contents promise to be of immediate service.[2]

Edward Tylor's letter is more guarded, intentionally, as his later references to Morgan indicate:

Some weeks ago I received a copy of your great work on "Systems of Consanguinity and Affinity" and while waiting to ascertain whether it was to yourself or the Smithsonian Institution that I was indebted for this magnificent treatise, your recent Australian pamphlet reached me sent by you. (I see by this that you have become acquainted with Mr. McLennan's remarkable dissertation.) Pray accept my best thanks for these gifts of which I assure you that I appreciate the great value as bearing on the difficult problem of early social rela-

[1] Dated Down, Beckenham, Kent, January 20, 1872.

[2] Dated Bayswater, London, February 16, 1872.

tions. I shall hope to make use of your research in a work on the Morals and Politics of the Lower Races, but it will be years first. As yet the only books of yours which I have profited by is the "Iroquois League."

The Smithsonian Institution has set the world an example in facilitating the circulation of scientific materials. It is to be hoped that the plan will become universal so that every worker will have easy means of knowing what has been done already in his line, and start at the most advanced point. I am glad to see your work published under the auspices of the Institution. It may interest you to hear that our Anthropological Institute has passed out of its state of civil war and may be expected to do excellent work in years to come.[1]

G. Staniland Wake, the English anthropologist, responded to Morgan's note commenting on his review of the book:

Your letter has reached me here and I am very glad to find from it that you think that I have treated your work on Consanguinity, with fairness. I endeavored to do so, but the subject is so new, and you have brought together so many facts that I might well have unintentionally left out of sight questions necessary for a right discussion of it. You would observe that my argument is that the existence of a condition of promiscuity has not been proved, in fact, that the evidence is wanting to support it, but I am quite ready to be convinced should the evidence be forthcoming. This may be in the work which I am glad to hear you are preparing and which I have no doubt will throw great light on the social condition of primeval man, or shall we say primitive man, as there is no knowing what changes may have taken place since the first appearance of man on the earth. No doubt you know the opinion expressed by Sir Henry

[1] Dated Linden, Wellington, Somerset, January 28, 1873.

Maine that many of the apparently primitive customs of the hill tribes of India are of comparatively recent introduction.

I am myself bringing out a work which is now passing through the press on the development of morality which I trust may be of some service in aiding in the understanding of man's early social state, a subject in which as an anthropologist, I take a profound interest.

Your estimation of their work will be highly appreciated by my scientific colleagues and shall be reported to them.[1]

Henry Maine's letter contrasts his approach with that of Morgan and shows him to be receptive to the latter's contribution:

I have carefully followed all your investigations so far as they are known to me and in my last book I have spoken of the value of your Systems of Consanguinity and Affinity. I hear with much pleasure that you have a volume in the press.

As you truly say, we have attacked the same subject from opposite sides. I understand you to have begun with observations of the customs of savages whereas I began as a Professor of Jurisprudence and should very probably have never interested myself in primitive usage, if I had not been profoundly discontented with the modes of explaining legal rules which were in practice when I began to write. I am still apt to limit my enquiries to ancient institutions which I can more or less distinctly connect with modern ideas and ways of thought.

No doubt the two lines of enquiry promise more and more to connect themselves together, and if I am not yet prepared to say that the connection has been established, I am quite ready to be convinced whenever the

[1] Dated Hull, England, January 19, 1873.

evidence is sufficient. Your work on Systems of Consanguinity etc. carried the evidence much farther than before, and I shall look forward with much curiosity to your new publication. No doubt the history of property is greatly bound up with that of social development, and I suspect that physiology and biology must be called in before all is clear. I myself stumble a little at the unquestioning acceptance by anthropologists of the theological assumption of the descent of mankind from the single pair which seems to pervade a good deal of present investigation of savage customs.[1]

Morgan did not receive such sympathetic treatment in the hands of the two other leading English anthropologists, John Lubbock and John F. McLennan, and the controversy begun by these men was waged for many years with much acrimony. Lubbock spoke well of Morgan's work in his presidential address before the Anthropological Institute of Great Britain and Ireland in 1871; and although he rearranged Morgan's data and differed with him over some of his conclusions, he stated:

Mr. Morgan, whose remarkable memoir, entitled "A Conjectural Solution of the Origin of the Classificatory System of Relationship" is doubtless well known to many gentlemen present, has now published, by the assistance of the Smithsonian Institution, his promised work on the same subject. Those who have read his preliminary memoir, will naturally have waited for the full development of his views, as well as of the facts on which they are based, with much interest; and they will not be disappointed, for Mr. Morgan's work is certainly one of the most valuable contributions to ethnological science which has appeared for many years.[2]

[1] Dated London, July 30, 1876.

[2] *Journal of the Anthropological Institute*, 1871, pp. 1 *et seq.*

Later he criticized Morgan's findings, but said:

I do not, however, in any way undervalue their importance; they afford a striking evidence in favour of the doctrine of development, and are thus a very interesting and important contribution to the great problem of human history.[1]

The reviewer of the book in *Nature* took occasion to contrast Morgan's views with those of Lubbock's to the disadvantage of the former. Morgan, resentful of the criticism, attempted to answer Lubbock through the columns of *Nature;* and when Lubbock rejoined, he retorted.[2] The controversy roused the friends of Morgan. Asa Gray wrote from Harvard:

I am reading *Nature* of June 3.
I thought you would notice the flippant criticism referred to. The review is a specimen of many in England, and I am glad you notice it. By sufficient raps on the knuckles we may at length teach our cousins over the water decent attention to what they write about and manners. I am surprised that Lubbock should have either misrepresented or misunderstood. He should know better.[3]

To this letter Morgan replied at length:

I received your letter referring to my article in Nature answering Sir John Lubbock's reviewer with much pleasure. You probably noticed Lubbock's answer in the number of June 17 and my reply in August 19.
I hope this will be the end of it for I have no relish for such controversies. If he replies I think I shall go no further. He has misunderstood my book very carelessly.

[1] *The Origin of Civilisation*, p. 161.
[2] *Nature*, XI, 401–3; XII, 86, 124, 311.
[3] Dated Cambridge, Massachusetts, June 27, 1875.

I have a new book nearly ready entitled *Ancient Society or Researches on the Lines of Human Progress through Savagery and Barbarism to Civilization* in which the principle results in the volume on Consanguinity are more fully extended and explained. What little I have done, and it is not much, I expect to keep against all claimants.

One or two more generations will give us a race of American scholars who will equal and I believe excel those of England, France and Germany and do much of their own work over for them. They beat us at present by numbers, by stricter professional education and by devoting more years of labor to special subject. But the mental power expended upon the material resources of United States in the last hundred years is unparalleled in human experience, and when it turns upon the departments of science on which its work has already commenced I believe in the final triumph of American genius and thought in the affairs of the earth and am gradually losing my reverence for European thought and logic which is now great among our scholars.[1]

The irascible McLennan, said to have been piqued because he felt that Morgan had used his work without proper acknowledgment, attacked *Systems of Consanguinity*, declaring it to be "a wild dream, not to say nightmare of early institutions," and persisted in pouring vitriol against Morgan until he died. His attack on this book, brought a letter from Professor Henry:

I have read the work on *Primitive Marriage* and have come to the same conclusion which you have in regard to the aggressive and unjust criticism the author has bestowed upon your work. Before receiving your letter I had concluded to write to him to thank him for the

[1] Dated Rochester, September 15, 1875.

copy of his work to express the pleasure and profit I had derived from the reading of it but to dissent from the character and unjustness of his criticism of your work.

I am entirely satisfied that your tables are very valuable additions to the positive materials on which the •past history of the human race is to be constructed.

Whatever deductions may be drawn from them or whatever hypotheses may be adopted in regard to the explanation they must always be considered as embodying a series of facts which must not be gainsaid.

I have, it is true, been much struck by the plausibility of the hypothesis assumed by Mr. McLennan—first of the struggle of existence leading to infanticide of females, the consequent capturing of wives, the introduction of polyandria and the consequent descent of relationship through the female and the final descent through the male by modified polyandria in which the wife is common to a family of brothers.

The whole is a very plausible hypothesis, but I do not see why all your facts are not in accordance with it.[1]

The *Independent* quoted a comment from the *Revue scientifique* and used Morgan's book in an attempt to discredit radical groups:

"We have seen in our day," adds the *Revue scientifique* "that the reformers of the *Internationale* regard free love as tending to replace marriage." Thus promiscuous intercourse occurs at the two extremes of the history of human beings: accidently and due to savage violence at first; and finally as in the French Communists, and we might add, sporadically in the United States, it becomes elective and a matter of choice. There is nothing more interesting in the science of man than the history of the formation of the family, which the works of Bachofen, MacLennen, Cordier, Morgan and Lubbock are elaborating. While a certain class of "reformers" are under-

[1] Dated Smithsonian Institution, Washington, D.C., February 14, 1877.

mining the family relation, Dr. Allen is pointing out the physical degeneracy of the race in New England.[1]

A later reviewer ventured the opinion that "the book is operose and fanciful and of the Smithsonian publications it is easiest to do without."[2]

III

In judging the value of *Systems of Consanguinity*, we must distinguish three aspects of the work, viz.: the accumulation of the materials, the arrangement of the materials, and the conclusions reached by Morgan as a result of the investigation..

In the first instance, critical judgment is unanimous in declaring the book to be a very valuable addition to the source materials of primitive society, and the prodigious labor involved in their accumulation is worthy of high praise. The data have been and are used repeatedly to good advantage by ethnologists. In his recent work on the subject[3] Leslie Spier acknowledges having derived much of his data from the book. The arrangement of the material was, however, not especially fortunate. Lubbock, in the address previously mentioned, felt obliged to reclassify the materials as have all anthropologists who have made use of them.

Morgan distinguished between the "descriptive" and the "classificatory" systems of kinship terms. He cited, as representative of the "descriptive" type, the "Aryan," "Semitic," and the "Uralian" systems, and thought it to be inevitably bound up with monogamy and the in-

[1] *Independent*, New York, November 9, 1871.

[2] *American* (Philadelphia), III, January 7, 1882, p. 198.

[3] *The Distribution of Kinship Systems in North America.*

stitution of the modern family and therefore employed by all or most of the peoples who had attained civilization. The classificatory system, which required for its origin a form of "group marriage," he considered coextensive with savagery and barbarism and representative of an earlier stage of development. The American Indian systems and primitive nomenclatures as a whole were therefore used to illustrate the second type.

Kroeber,[1] Rivers,[2] and Lowie[3] have been the severest critics of Morgan's classification. Kroeber and Rivers have pointed out that the kinship terms "cousin" and "uncle" in English and other Indo-European terminologies are classificatory, an inconsistency which Morgan noted and tried unsuccessfully to explain as being due to "the constantly recurring desire to avoid the inconvenience of descriptive phrases."[4] Kroeber points out that the distinction which Morgan makes between the two classes or systems of indicating relationship is subjective and has its origin in the point of view of investigators, who, on approaching foreign languages, have been impressed with their failure to discriminate certain relationships between which the European languages distinguish. In formulating general theories from such facts, they neglect analogous groupings and classifications in their own languages which they accept without critical analysis because custom has made them so familiar. Kroeber summarizes:

[1] *Journal of the Anthropological Institute*, XXXIX, 77–83.

[2] *Anthropological Essays Presented to E. B. Tylor*, pp. 309–23.

[3] *American Anthropologist*, N.S., XXX, 263–67.

[4] *Systems of Consanguinity*, pp. 12, 48.

Judged from its own point of view, English is the less classificatory; looked at from the Indian point of view, it is the more classificatory, inasmuch as in every one of its terms it fails to recognize certain distinctions often made in other languages; regarded from a general and comparative point of view, neither system is more or less classificatory. In short, the prevalent idea of the classificatory system breaks down entirely under analysis.[1]

Lowie calls attention to the fact that "classificatory" and "descriptive" are not complementary concepts but belong to different logical universes, and that therefore the arrangement of the data in these categories is erroneous regardless of the relevant facts.[2]

As indicated previously, Morgan hoped to prove the ethnic relationship of those groups which had like kinship systems. He failed utterly to make the basic distinction between cultural heritage and biological heritage, and his failure led him to absurd conclusions. He believed, for example, that "the custom of saluting by kin, the usage of wearing the breech-cloth and the usage of sleeping at night in a state of nudity, each person being wrapped in a separate covering," are "transmitted with the blood" and indicate the unity of origin of the peoples practicing them. The fact that peoples in cold climates retained the "breech-cloth," which was adapted to tropical climates, proved for him the "difficulty of casting off, under changed conditions, these blood or hereditary usages."[3] It was his indecision in

[1] Kroeber, *op. cit.*, p. 80.

[2] Lowie, *op. cit.*, p. 264.

[3] *Systems of Consanguinity*, pp. 274–75, n. 1.

this book on the question whether the kinship system
were "natural," i.e., biological, or "artificial" cultural
inventions which led to his controversy with Lubbock.
He inclined toward the preposterous belief that they
were the former, a belief which he clung to with minor
qualifications in his later works. He puts forth his proposition in the Preface:

Whether as organic forms they are capable of crossing
the line of demarcation which separates one family from
another, and of yielding evidence of the ethnic connection of such families, will depend upon the stability of
these forms and their power of self-perpetuation in the
streams of the blood through indefinite periods of time.
For the purpose of determining, by ample tests, whether
these systems possess such attributes, the investigation
has been extended over a field sufficiently wide to embrace four-fifths and upwards of the human family.[1]

He contends early in the book:

Special features, such as these, incorporated in a system of relationship, are of great value for ethnological
purposes. Where not essentially foreign to the system
that may be explained as deviations from uniformity
which sprang up fortuitously in a particular branch of a
great family of nations, after which they were transmitted with the blood to the subdivisions of such
branch; or, if fundamentally different from the original
system of the family, they may have resulted from a
combination of two radically distinct forms, and therefore, indicate a mixture of the blood of two peoples be-
longing to different families. They are worthy of investigation for the possible information they may yield
upon the question of the blood affinities of nations which
concur in their possession, however widely separated

[1] *Ibid.*, p. 6.

they may be from each other. If the divergent element is unexplainable as a development from the materials of the common system of the family, its foreign origin, through mixture of blood, will become a strong presumption.[1]

It is significant in the light of the theory of independent origin commonly associated with his name that he here rejects the hypothesis that like systems of consanguinity could have arisen "by spontaneous growth in like disconnected areas, under the influences of suggestions springing from similar wants in similar conditions of society" as a "violent hypothesis." He favors the hypothesis of their "transmission with the blood from a common original source," as both "adequate and satisfactory":

If it is assumed then that the Turanian and the Ganowanian [Morgan's word for the American Indian based on the Iroquois words for bow and arrow] were created independently in Asia and America, would each by imperative necessity have passed through the same experience, have developed the same sequence of customs and institutions, and, as a final result, have produced the same identical system of relationship? The statement of the proposition seems to work its refutation on the grounds of its excessive improbability . . . If the two families commenced on separate continents in a state of promiscuous intercourse, . . . it would be little less than a miracle if both should develop the same ultimate system of relationship. Upon the doctrine of chances it is not supposable that each would pass through the same experience, develop the same series of customs and institutions and finally produce for them-

[1] *Ibid.*, p. 43.

selves the same system of consanguinity, which would be found, on comparison, to be identical in radical characteristics as well as coincident in minute details. . . . .

The system once established finds in the diverging streams of the blood an instrument and a means for its transmission through periods of indefinite duration. As these innumerable lines ascend through the ages they converge continually until they finally meet in a common point, and whatever was in the original blood, capable of flowing in its currents, was as certain to be transmitted as the blood itself. Could anything have existed in the ancient human brain more likely to follow down in these streams of existence, through all vicissitudes, than those simple ideas in their fixed relations by which man sought to distinguish his several kinsmen? These ideas were seeds planted in the beginning and perpetually germinating.[1]

His final conclusion is that because the people of India and the Americas had the same systems of consanguinity, they were biologically related, and that therefore he had contributed proof to the hypothesis of the Asiatic origin of the American Indian:

When the discoverers of the New World bestowed upon its inhabitants the name of Indians under the impression that they had reached the Indies, they little suspected that children of the same original family, although upon a different continent, stood before them. By a singular coincidence error was truth.[2]

It was his belief that the source of migration in Asia was the Amur River Valley, and that the incursion to the American continent was by way of the Aleutian

[1] *Ibid.*, pp. 504–5.   [2] *Ibid.*, p. 588.

Chain to the Columbia River Valley. This he held to be the "nursery of the Ganowanian family"—the initial point of migration from which both North and South America received their inhabitants.[1] The migration he thought long subsequent to the development of the tribal organization.

As Morgan's hypothesis concerning the sequence of kinship institutions are here in their embryonic form and are developed more fully in *Ancient Society*, his conclusions on this aspect of the work will be considered in the critical analysis of that book.

[1] *Ibid.*, p. 498. Cf. his "Indian Migrations," *North American Review*, CIX, 391–442; CX, 33–82.

CHAPTER IV

ANIMAL PSYCHOLOGY

As early as 1843, Morgan expressed his interest in animal psychology in an extended article in *Knickerbocker*, a New York periodical. In this contribution entitled, "Mind or Instinct: An Inquiry Concerning the Manifestation of Mind by the Lower Animals,"[1] he contended that man erroneously claims the exclusive possession of "the Thinking Principle." He challenged man to compare his accomplishments in "a state of nature" with those of the lower animals instead of judging the relative intelligence of man and animal on the basis of man's present civilized status. He ascribed the animals' lack of material improvement in different generations to the fact that they "generally require no artificial means to promote their happiness, neither have they the gregarious principle to the same extent as man."

The primary object of his inquiry was to ascertain by an examination of animal behavior "whether the principle called Instinct manifests the same intellectual qualities as Mind, without having any reference to its *moral* attributes." He expatiated on the vagueness of the concept of animal instinct and then presented "the utmost number of ways in which the manifestations of instinct are analogous to the manifestation of mind as exhibited by the human race." This he did under four general headings, I, "Of the Memory of the Principle

[1] November and December, 1843, pp. 414–20, 507–15.

Called Instinct"; II, "Of the Process of Abstraction by Instinct"; III, "Of the Imagination of the Principle Called Instinct"; IV, "Of the Reason or Judgment of the Principle Called Instinct." He quoted extensively from Buffon's *Natural History* illustrations of memory, abstraction, imagination, and reason exhibited by animals, supplementing these by other tales of the exploits of animals from Pliny, Virgil, Aesop, and others, all of which accounts he accepted uncritically. His conclusion was syllogistic, "That Principle which remembers, abstracts, imagines and reasons is Mind. The Principle called Instinct remembers, abstracts, imagines and reasons. Therefore, this Principle is Mind." He recognized man's relation to the lower animals:

The history of animals and man exhibits so many characteristics in common and those which we have discovered only in men, merely serving to establish endowments stronger in degree without warranting a fundamental distinction, that a scale of intelligence from man to the most inferior animal appears to result as naturally as a scale of intelligence among men, founded on their different characteristics.

But he saw design in the universe and a pleasure-pain motivation in all behavior:

. . . . the same thinking intellectual Principle pervades all animated existences; created by the Deity and bestowed in such measures upon the different species as appeared in his wisdom requisite for the destiny and happiness of each. . . . . We are alike all creatures of the Deity and subjects of His will. He designed all existence. He bestowed it and His beneficent protection over all his works.

His work in connection with his railroad on the shores of Lake Superior near Marquette enabled Morgan to make some original investigations to test out his beliefs on the intelligence of animals. First in 1855, and during many summers thereafter, he spent his spare hours in this region observing the fascinating habits of the beaver. In 1861, on his visit to the Red River settlement in the Hudson's Bay Territory, and in 1862, when he ascended the Missouri River to the Rocky Mountains, he compared the works of the beaver in these localities with those on Lake Superior. His interest having been thoroughly awakened, he took careful and extensive notes on his observations. These he published in 1868 with the addition of two chapters on the anatomy of the beaver by a Rochester friend, Dr. W. W. Ely, under the title, *The American Beaver and His Work.*

Morgan captioned his book with a pertinent quotation from Agassiz: "And after all, what does it matter to science that thousands of species, more or less, should be described and entered in our systems, if we know nothing about them." He held that zoölogy had not fulfilled its task when its exposition was limited to the frigid details of anatomical structure, for "each animal is endowed with a living and also with a thinking principle the manifestations of each of which are not less important and instructive than the mechanism of the material frames in which they reside." His objective was to depict the beavers' artificial works, their habits, their mode of life, and their mutual relations. He described their method of constructing dams, lodges, burrows, canals, meadows, and trails, their means of subsistence, and the modes of trapping them. He manifested in this work his aptness for intelligent and accurate observation and his ability to document his findings meticulously.

The final chapter of the book, which is a revision of an address on animal psychology which he delivered before "The Club" in 1857, opens with a sharp criticism of "metaphysicians" who are perpetually hesitant in recognizing that animals manifest the same characteristics displayed by humans "lest the high position of man should be shaken or impaired." He declared it to be difficult, in right reason, to discover the slightest tendency to lower the personal dignity of man, or to alter in the least his responsibility to God, by recognizing the existence in the mutes of a thinking, self-conscious principle, the same in kind that man possesses but feebler in degree; nor even by conceding their possession of a moral sense, although, so far as our present knowledge extends, it is so faintly developed as scarcely to deserve the name. Man at least should neither admit or deny the moral sense to lower animals because of the supposed bearing of such an admission upon his own relations to the Supreme Being.[1]

The word "instinct," which in his "Club" address he had attacked as a "fraud upon the animal races . . . . an installation of the supernatural which silences at once all inquiry into the facts," he here characterized as "a vague fictitious invention of these metaphysicians for the purpose of retaining the chasm between man and the animal, which leaves the phenomena unexplained . . . . an arbitrary term . . . . an evasion of the true question

[1] *The American Beaver*, p. 248.

involved."[1] And again: "As a term or invention it is *functus officio*. With its disuse the subject of Animal Psychology is freed from all extraneous embarrassments."[2]

His argument proceeds:

.... the Creator .... intrusted to each individual species a principle of intelligence .... endowed [each] with a mental or spiritual essence which is distinct from the body, but associated with it in a mysterious manner. .... [This] manifests certain faculties, as memory, certain passions, as anger, certain appetites, as hunger, and puts forth a certain power, the will in both animal and man alike. Man owes his superior dignity not to the exclusive possession of this principle but rather to its enjoyment in a higher, more ample and more distinguishing degree .... [due to] one of the extraordinary features of this Divine gift that it is capable of adaptation to so many and to such diversified organisms .... and still the fundamental similarities of its common principle through all its ramifications.[3]

He evaded the question of whether the mutes possess "a conscience or the moral sense" as being incapable of solution, and found untenable "the artificial distinction .... made between the appetites and passions on the one hand and intellectual powers on the other" on the basis of "an axiom in moral as well as in intellectual science, that pain and pleasure are experienced in the mind and not in the organs of the body." He then argued, in a manner which might generously be called the method of comparative psychology, that the similar structural organization, the like possession of "the prin-

[1] *Ibid.*, p. 248.   [2] *Ibid.*, p. 276.   [3] *Ibid.*, pp. 249 *et seq.*

ciple of life" or self-consciousness, the manifestations of memory, reason or judgment, imagination, the will, appetites and passions by animals, and finally "lunacy" of animals, prove: first, that the term "instinct," to explain the intelligent acts of animals, should be abandoned; second, that animals are "endowed with a mental principle which performs for them the same office that the human mind does for man"; and third, that the difference in the behavior of man and animal "is one of degree and not of kind . . . . that the principle from which they emanate is the same in kind, but bestowed in different measure to adapt each species to its particular mode of life."[1]

Although Darwin's *Origin of Species* had appeared in 1859, Morgan does not mention it here, and showed no knowledge of its existence. He still believed in the special creation of each species even though he recognized similarities among the species. Likewise, although he conceded man's relationship with the lower animals, he wrote:

The hiatus between man and the nearest species below him in the scale of intelligence is so wide as to disturb the symmetrical gradation of the several order of animals. We can neither conjecture that some intermediate order has fallen out of existence, nor assume the permanent degradation of any existing species; but on the contrary, it seems to have been part of the original plan of creation that man should stand without a compeer or contestant, the indisputable head of the series of organic forms, and the recipient in the largest measure, of the gift of the mental principle.[2]

[1] *Ibid.*, pp. 252–84.   [2] *Ibid.*, p. 279.

Morgan's criticism of the use of the word "instinct" anticipated modern psychology more closely than did Darwin's analysis of instinct in his *Descent of Man*, where he paid tribute to Morgan's study of the beaver but remarked, "I cannot help thinking, however, that he goes too far in underrating the power of instinct."[1]

Morgan also anticipated the conclusions of later scientists when he attributed man's ability to accumulate culture to language. After speaking of man's advance from his primitive condition, he wrote:

Language has been the great instrument of this progress, the power of which was increased many fold when it clothed itself in written characters. He was thus enabled to perpetuate the results of individual experience and transmit them through the ages. Each discovery thus became a foundation on which to mount up to new discoveries.[2]

But that he did not clearly recognize the distinction between the organic and the cultural is evident from his immediate discussion of the progress of animals:

Within the period of human observation, their progress has seemed to be inconsiderable—but yet not absolutely nothing. For example, dogs under training have developed special capacities, such as the pointer and the setter, and have transmitted them to their offspring. This shows not only progress, but that of so marked a character as to work a transformation in the characteristics of the animal. Many animals, as the elephant, the horse, the bear, and even the hog—the type of stupidity—have been taught a variety of performances, under the stimulus of rewards, of which they were previously ignorant. These examples, however are less im-

[1] *Descent of Man*, p. 84.   [2] *The American Beaver*, p. 280.

portant than the knowledge acquired by undomesticated animals and transmitted as part of their experience and knowledge, in the species in which they were acquired.[1]

In spite of his keen criticism of the use of the word "instinct," in which he anticipates contemporary scientific views, Morgan's writings on this subject are permeated with the faculty psychology; and he does not divorce himself from the conventional, theological, and teleological setting of his epoch. His "thinking principle" partakes the character of Platonic archetypal idea, and the concept of design in the universe pervades his views.

The *American Beaver* was very favorably reviewed by Jefferies Wyman of Harvard in the *Nation* and also in the *Atlantic Monthly*.[2] It was through it that his friendship arose with Wendell Phillips Garrison, the editor of the *Nation*, who, impressed with Morgan's discussion of instinct, asked him to review for the *Nation* Chadbourne's book *Instinct: Its Office in the Animal Kingdom and Its Relation to the Higher Powers in Man*. Morgan, in his review of this book, stated his position succinctly:

Dr. Chadbourne adopts the *"instinct hypothesis"* to explain the phenomena of animal intelligence, and regards it as adequate to embrace and account for all the facts. Having adopted this hypothesis in the title of his work (which hypothesis it would be pleasant to ascribe to human laziness, if it could properly be done), he was substantially released from the necessity of collecting and discussing the vast and complicated array of facts revealed by the lives of lower animals.

[1] *Ibid.*, p. 281.

[2] *Nation*, February 27, 1868, p. 176; *Atlantic Monthly*, April, 1868, p. 512.

He attacked all the definitions of instinct which Chadbourne presented as leading directly

to the Cartesian theory that every animal below man is
a mere machine—a living machine it is true—actuated
by a power analogous to the mainspring of a watch, over
which the animal has no control. . . . . It is a modern
invention of the metaphysicians to dispose of the whole
subject of animal psychology by definition, and to create
by force of a term, a fundamental distinction between
the endowments of man and of animals where there is
no sufficient reason for supposing that any difference
exists except in degree. It is a mere theory or hypothesis,
with an object, strange to say having but a limited relation to the facts.[1]

Morgan's views on instincts appear to have had little
influence upon later writers on the subject of animal
psychology, who, until recently, have persisted in using
the term with many of the implications to which Morgan correctly objected. His contribution in this field has
therefore not received the acknowledgment that it deserves in the literature of animal psychology. His name-
sake, C. Lloyd Morgan, has dominated the field.

[1] *Nation*, May 2, 1872, pp. 291–92.

CHAPTER V

CRITIQUE OF THE MEXICAN ANNALISTS

Morgan's recognition in America by his contemporaries came primarily through his work on a critical reconstruction of the culture of Mexico and Central America. As early as 1856, probably under the influence of Albert Gallatin[1] and Lewis Cass,[2] he had attacked the accounts of the "pretended crown of Mexico or Aztec monarchy," and had criticized the records of the Spanish conquest and Prescott's recital of them as being full of contradictory assertions, gross exaggerations, and fabulous statements. The contention which he presented at that time permeates all his later writings on this subject:

Now the institutions of all the aboriginal races of the continent have a family cast. They bear internal evidence of common paternity, and point to a common origin but remote as to time and place. They sprang from a common mind, and that their progressive developments have still retained the impress of original elements is abundantly verified. The Aztecs were thoroughly and essentially Indian. We have glimpses here and there of original institutions which suggest at once by their similarity kindred ones among the Iroquois and other Indian races of the present day. . . . . Differences existed it is true, but they were not radical. The Aztec civilization simply exhibited a more advanced develop-

[1] *Transactions of American Ethnological Society,* Vol. I.

[2] *North American Review,* October, 1840, pp. 396–433.

ment of those primary ideas of civil and social life which were common to the whole Indian family. . . . .

. . . . Montezuma so far from being the emperor of the Aztecs, was one of a large number of sachems, who equally by their joint authority in council administered the affairs of the commonwealth . . . . as leading sachem residing in the metropolitan city, he was first brought in contact with the Spaniard.[1]

His interest in the problem of aboriginal Mexican life persisted; and he sought data concerning the material culture of the region by communicating with residents of the Southwest, obtaining from them measurements of the dwellings of the Indians. He received encouragement from Francis Parkman, who wrote him in 1865:

I fully agree with you as to the possibility of deriving very important results from the analysis and comparison of Indian practices and institutions. My own examinations have been made with an historical not an ethnological object, though I have always felt much interest in the ethnological aspect of the subject. . . . . All that I have been able to discover strongly inclines me to the belief that the natives of Mexico and Peru are radically of the one family with our Northern Indians, though I cannot say that I have reached as yet a clear conviction.[2]

He wrote again in 1867,

As to the Mexicans, I am wholly of your mind. That whole investigation must be done over again by one who studies them among their descendants and their monuments, discarding the romance of the annalists, and resolutely searching out the facts. Their civilization,

[1] *Proceedings of the 11th Meeting of the American Association for the Advancement of Science*, Montreal, August, 1856, Sec. 2, pp. 132-48. Also published in 1858 under the title *Laws of Descent of the Iroquois*.

[2] Dated Boston, September 24, 1865.

such as it was, is too important a subject to be veiled in the romantic haze of fanciful chronicle.[1]

The architectural ruins of Mexico, Yucatan, and Central America had been compared by the earlier writers to the ruins of Thebes, Baalbec, Nineveh, and Babylon, to palaces and temples like the Alhambra and the Parthenon. In an article entitled "Seven Cities of Cibola" in the *North American Review*, Morgan tried to burst the bubble of exaggeration that marked these popular descriptions of Mexican dwellings as palatial residences of emperors, by interpreting them as communal dwellings in terms of the Iroquois "long-house."[2] This article, though reviewed in the *Nation*, did not attract much attention. Francis Parkman, however, commented:

I have been much interested in your investigations, especially in that of the "Seven Cities." You touch nothing on which you do not throw light. The more advanced we become in intellectual progress, the more your labors will be appreciated.[3]

In December, 1873, Adolph Bandelier, the erudite and erratic Swiss archaeologist, who later became Morgan's most militant advocate and defender on the Mexican controversy, followed a friendly introductory visit to Morgan with a letter which initiated an extensive correspondence between the two men. The letter portrays vividly the difference in the approach and opinions of the two men, how they supplemented each other's efforts, and the inception of Morgan's influence on Bandelier:

[1] Dated Boston, June 9, 1867.

[2] *North American Review*, CVIII, 457–98.

[3] Dated Boston, November 29, 1869.

. . . . You have warned me seriously against placing too much reliance on the statements of the older authors. I heed this warning at every step but still can we judge of the unadulterated condition of the American aborigines except by *their* statements? What we see now are only the crumbling ruins of a decayed race, doomed to perdition without hope, probably for an accumulation of moral sins persistently committed, for an abuse of powers and gifts bestowed upon them and all around them. We find them now with distorted tradition, waning before the light of a revolution that has subverted all their conceptions, habits and ideas. Within themselves the new is mixed with the old, recent *facts*, dimly understood, have become articles of mythological faith (*vide* the new-Mexican *God* Montezuma!). Their creed is shaken, step by step have they lost faith, practically in their holiest thoughts and desires. What can the present study of such a race give us, which would be of more *critical* value than are the statements of cultivated minds which observed the same race at the time of its purity and comparative strength? Are not both branches the ethnological (the present) and the historical (the past) to go rather parallel?

If I have not misunderstood you, the common terms of "monarchy," "empire," even of state and nation, could not be applied to the Indian society. Allow me now, in view of obtaining further enlightenment, to expose to you my conception of the state of things in America, about the year say, 1520 (as an illustration merely this date is given). With the exception of Virginia, I have not found yet in N.A. any shadow of a "state," the despotic rule of the Natchez, perhaps excepted. As to Virginia which some, very unjustly, have called the "Powhatan Confederacy," it was nothing else, or rather it *became,* in the course of the 16th Century, but the *germ* of a political amalgamation or centralised despotism that might have, in the course of time, played on the North American continent, a rôle analogous to the one assumed by the Yncas in S. America. But the English strangled the new-born child. Most fortunately, by the way. I do not place exceeding credit in the glowing descriptions of the "Gentleman of Elvas" of Antonio Beidma and of Rochefort, about the Maubilians, Apachians etc., for Cabeca du Vaca, who knew them better, speaks differently. The New Mexican pueblos were "communities" and not states. The remainder of the central western Indians are sufficiently characterised by the words of Antonio Beidma "like our Arabs. . . . ."

But in regard to Central America, Mexico in chief, I cannot help finding there, in truth a despotic barbarous monarchy, but still a monarchy, a political body, a state. That monarchy was hereditary at Tezcuco, at Michoacan, at Mexico it was hereditary as to dynasty, election ("por elección," says Herrera) as to the members thereof. And the extensive domination of that hereditary-elective chief, to whom the Spaniards themselves gave spontaneously the title of "King (El Rey Montezuma)" is among others clearly established by the testimony of his bitterest enemy, Ixtlitlxochitl (Historia Chichemeca) by Acosta, by Herrera, even by Cortez himself. (Carta terzia y quarta.) It is true there was only a local not a national spirit, prevailing in the state of Anahuac, but still it formed a body corporate and politic, though of only very recent and unstable formation.

In Yucatan, I am inclined to see the fragments of an original central despotism, shattered by revolution, and certainly declining in culture and arts. But a *state* in due form, a state after oriental barbarous types, though I find again in Guatemala, in Quiché (See among other, Herrera). I hold, until now, Quiché to be the oldest despotic realm of the western continent, older than any district of Mexico, older than the Ynca empire.

On the S. American continent, there appear to me two points, where political stability had continued. The one is the singular semi-religious Muysca-conglomerate in the Bogotan table-land, and the other is the great empire of the Yncas. Of the Muyscas I know but very little, the sources which I could consult being limited to Girolamo Benzoni's "Storia di Nuevo Mundo" (ab't 1559), Herrera and Humboldt "Vues Des Cordilleres etc.," besides some stray notices in the older works. But the impression conveyed is that the Muyscas had attained a degree of culture superior even to the Aztecs, an idea which an authority like Robertson would seem to confirm also.

As to the Yncas, aside from the question of their origin, the result speaks for itself. To bring under one head, an extent of country reaching from the Rio Manle to Chili, to the Rio Ancasmayu in Ecuador, a N.-S.'ly length of about 2000 miles, at least, to obliterate practically over that entire region, the *languages* of the different tribes, to transplant whole colonies of one tribe at a great distance, and to supply their place with others from different parts, to make the customs, nay the religion of the subjugated tribes even, subservient to the purposes of domination; that certainly indicates an intellectual development superior to many states of the old world. It is certainly *barbarous*, but it is an evidence of highly developed, though less moral mind. I take these facts from numerous Spanish fathers, and they are corroborated by the present remains in Peru. (See among recent authorities, which I am fully acquainted with, La Condamine, Humboldt, Tschudi and Rivero, Markham, Squier and LePlongeon.)

As to the other S. American tribes, there were agricultural "village" Indians, principally in Paraguay,

(Guaranis) and probably also among the Venezuelan coast as among the populous districts of Uraba and Cauca of New-Granada. The stability of dwellings in the latter was marred however by a fearful cannibalism. The greater portion of the rest were probably nomadic.

Excuse the lengthiness and also perhaps the too positive tone of the above. Please to interpret it only as it is meant to be given, as a statement of my *actual* position which if wrong, I should desire to have set right. And if your time should permit you, and if by the long though involuntary delay, I have not lost all claims upon your kindness, and you should be willing to put me right in these impressions, I should be again very much obliged and exceedingly thankful to you. . . . .[1]

It was at the instance of Henry Adams, who felt of Hubert H. Bancroft's *Native Races of the Pacific States of North America* that "it would be a disgrace to let such a work go out as a measure of our national scholarship," that Morgan launched his devastating attack on Bancroft's uncritical use of Spanish documents, which brought wide attention to his efforts. In a letter to F. W. Putnam, of Harvard, when submitting his article "Montezuma's Dinner," Morgan indicated his deep feeling on the subject and his motives in writing the article.

. . . . There was never a time in our country as I believe when the interest was stronger in the Indian subject than now: but as hithertofore the work is nearly all done by amateurs. Inflation and imaginary magnificence is the bane that infests all these efforts. But a better time is coming. At this moment we have no science of American Ethnology. The reason is the American material is enormous and it requires, as the

---

[1] Dated Highland, Illinois, December 20, 1873.

materials of any other science, twenty years of uninterrupted work in the field, and of thought and reflection, to master it. Among the young men now interested in the subject, we shall yet start a small number who will go beyond the mere amateur and go into the subject determined to know all about it. It has been my aim and object for years to get investigations started in the right direction. If we can but do that, the results that will come in at the end of a few more years will be splendid. They will be immense for the necessity of covering over European Ethnology for the Middle and for the Upper status of barbarism will be demonstrated.

Our first dead weight to be got rid of is the Aztec monarchy and the Aztec romance. The institutions of the Indian tribes, including the Aztec tribe, are especially democratical and the whole series of Spanish and American histories are delusive and fictitious, so far as Indian society and government are concerned. I have felt the dead weight of these accounts for years and have made a number of gentle remonstrances against it but regard for the memory of Prescott has retained my hand. The publication of Bancroft's *Native Races* alters the question. He has reiterated their worst exaggerations, their grossest absurdities and added glosses in advance of all of them. This work and the commendation it is receiving is nothing less than a crime against ethnological science. Every way it is lamentable: but it can be made an occasion for rising against the entire humbug and this good may come of it.

Henry Adams wrote me six months ago for a book notice of the *Native Races* which I declined for the reason that I had no time to read the book. After I got hold of the work and saw its makeup I felt the necessity of going in, and wrote to Adams that I would send him an article for the April number reviewing the second volume, if he wished it: but I sketched a plan on which I should do it and the radical character of the results. He asked me to do it nevertheless and yesterday I sent the article entitled "Montezuma's Dinner." It may be too pronounced for the Review. If it is published, I grant you to read it for it contains some general suggestions upon what must be done if we would make a scientific expedition of the social organizations, usages, customs and plan of life of the Indian tribes.[1]

"Montezuma's Dinner"[2] aroused much comment. F. W. Putnam, of Harvard, wrote:

How you have gone for Bancroft; you have taken his scalp off down to his neck. I think you have made a strong point there on the Pueblo question but I can hardly admit with you yet that the mound builders are the same, and I can hardly go the idea of the builders of the Palenque being of just the same race as the Iroquois. . . . .[3]

Later, upon receipt of Bandelier's paper on the "Art of War," the first of his contributions to back up Morgan's conclusions by a wide study of the Spanish sources,[4] Putnam commented in a letter to Morgan:

. . . . Mr. B. has evidently made a thorough study of the subject and has proved a pupil of whom you can well feel proud, for while he has adopted and carried out your views he has retained a manly independence which shows that he is working from his own convictions and thought guided by the hints you have given him. I was deeply interested in the paper and though it is hard to have the bottoms knocked out of the great American centres of civilization as has now been done for Mexico

[1] Dated Rochester, January 29, 1876.
[2] *North American Review*, CXXII, 265-308.
[3] Dated Cambridge, August 5, 1876.
[4] *Reports of Peabody Museum*, Nos. X–XII.

and Peru, we must be thankful that the data exists for a better understanding than we have had before and that such men as Morgan and Bandelier are living and ready for the work. My own work has been so entirely from objects and not from books that I find much in all you and he write that is confirmatory of what I do from specimens as to prove that careful work from both these sources will in time clear up much which is now dark and mysterious. My great question now is: What connection existed between the early races of Central America and Peru? There are certainly some things in common and in Peru there seems to have been an early race far in advance of the socalled Inca tribe, for I get a development of art from Lake Titicaca that is far ahead of the coast civilization (if I may use the term) as "Etruscan" is over that of the Mound Builders of the Ohio Valley. I have also a very interesting point showing a probable connection between Central America and Peru in some form: viz a Llama in stone and clay from Nicaragua, and I notice that Mr. B. calls attention to the resemblances between the carvings on Palenque and the descriptions of dress and armor of the war chief of Mexico. . . . .[1]

Henry Barnard reacted to "Montezuma's Dinner" thus:

You have done for the student of our aboriginal history what Mommsen did for Rome; you not only expose the errors and speculation of the early chronicles but you give us clear sunlight in which to walk with certain steps over so much that was obviously enough absurd, but which most of us could never clear up. . . . .[2]

David J. Miller, then in the Pueblo region, indorsed Morgan's position:

[1] Dated Cambridge, December 18, 1876.

[2] Dated Hartford, December 30, 1876.

.... I entirely agree with you in your theory as to the *facts of the case* concerning the life and times of the famous Aztec Montezuma, the popular accounts whereof furnished by all the historians are, as I have often thought so wholly imaginative and highly colored, and in very truth so disgusting on that account. .... I was gratified to find on reading your article that an authority learned in Indian ethnology had at length appeared, presenting to the world by statement and argument the true facts through a channel of the most respectable and effective, short of the book which I hope he will yet write in the interests of the truth of history.

.... as to Montezuma I presume the author [Bancroft] has but reproduced the accounts as he uniformly found them, the only marvel being that, learned in *Indianology* as he is presumed to be and no doubt really is, he should have believed them. The Pueblo Indians around us here in New Mexico and the Pueblo Indians of ancient Tenochtitlan, in old Mexico when Montezuma was there were and are, I have no doubt, the same in all their characteristics, very nearly—and we who see them and their long established government and manners and customs constantly, can much better than those who have never seen either, perceive and appreciate the absurdity of the romantic book accounts referred to. .... [1]

The article provoked an extended correspondence with Henry Adams, whose letters reveal the status of anthropology at the time, his own orientation in the field, his eager quest for data, and his intelligent discernment of the important implications of the inquiry:

.... I was much gratified with your "Montezuma's Dinner" which gave me a strong desire to ask you many

[1] Dated Santa Fe, New Mexico, July 2, 1876.

questions. My own lectures and instruction at Cambridge turn on the origin of political and legal institutions, especially in the German race. I am very curious to know whether our American Indians had any trace of the political and judicial organisation which characterises the earliest Germans known to us. Had they any legal modes of obtaining compensation for personal injuries? Had they any notion of suit at law? Had they any means of recovering lost or stolen property when found in the possession of other persons? Had they a court of law or a legal procedure?

My own suspicion is that the American Indian represents a stage of society antecedent to all this, and I so understand your views. But I would like to have all the information that can be got on the subject.

I had a warm argument with Mr. Francis Parkman not long since, on the inferences to be drawn from the astonishing similarity between the communal and family institutions of the American Indians and of the Indo-European races, which taken in connection with their theology and system of ancestor-worship forced me to the conviction that the stock must have been common from which they sprang. Parkman thought not, on the ground that human nature was uniform in its development. I care little which theory is adopted. One is for scientific hypotheses as good as the other. But I wish it might be settled which of the two shall be used as *the* scientific hypothesis.[1]

. . . . I would like to ask you some day when you are at leisure, to tell me whether in your opinion the Aryan family, the Semitic, etc., had already before their separation, and before the occupation of America by our Indians, passed through any yet simpler stage of Society or whether the stage we see in their common characteristics is simple enough to have served as the starting

[1] Dated Boston, April 29, 1876.

point. You will no doubt have dealt with this subject in your book. I hope to find my perplexity removed there.[1]

.... Apropos to the question in my last 'letter, I meant to ask whether you thought there was any opportunity to intercalate any stage of social development between absolute savagery (brutality) and the stage of our Indians. Are we to consider our Indians as in the first stage of social development, or in the second or third? And if there was any preceding stage, what were the characteristics which marked it? Communal institutions, ancestral and sun worship, family customs, and private redress sanctioned by public opinion, are the first germs of society that I can as yet see. Is it possible to imagine a still ruder stage before reaching the Fijians and the Digger Indians?[2]

.... My own point of view is so different from yours that I am unable to offer any suggestions that would be useful. I am clear however, that our American ethnology is destined to change the fashionable European theories of history to no small extent.

Can you tell me where I can find any information on the customs regulating marriage among our Indians. I see you state that their marriage permitted separation at will of either party. This implies that the wife remained after marriage under the general protection of her own family, and was not a member of her husband's family. If this can be proved I should be glad to know the facts.[3]

Albert Gatschet, the linguist, differed from Morgan in his generalization of primitive aboriginal democracy as applied to Mexico:

[1] Dated Boston, May 4, 1876.

[2] Dated Beverly Farms, Massachusetts, May 21, 1876.

[3] Dated Beverly Farms, Massachusetts, June 3, 1876.

. . . . Though there is truth in what you remark, I would in opposition say that many of the Southern Indians had far more aristocratical institutions than the northern—as the Natchez, Toltecs, Incas, Aztecs, etc. The term *liege, lord, vassals*, etc. should be suppressed indeed, though they are found in the historians who found no other institutions to compare with those they had known in Europe. The Timucua chieftainship must have been more absolute than that of the Northern Indians, for like that of the Natchez, it was *hereditary*, and the diverse clans, who were not allowed to intermarry, derived all their origin from the present or earlier head chiefs.[1]

Morgan followed up "Montezuma's Dinner" with an article on the "Houses of the Mound Builders," based on a paper which he had previously delivered before the American Association for the Advancement of Science.[2] Here Morgan attempted to show a relationship between the Mound Builders and the Mexicans.[3] Of these two articles Francis Parkman wrote:

I wish we had you in Cambridge. There are the beginnings of an archeological museum here and I hope that something will come of it. I was much interested in "Montezuma's Dinner" and the "Houses of the Mound Builders" and have no doubt whatever that the Mexican tribes were only tribes, and that the truth concerning them has been hidden by high flown phrases and misconception and the mendacity of the old writers. I shall look for your book with great interest. I have just printed one of my own, historical and not ethnological. . . . .

[1] Dated Washington, January 16, 1877.

[2] *North American Review*, CXXIII, 60–85.

[3] His conclusions on the Mound Builders are shown to be untenable by W. De Hass, *Smithsonian Miscellaneous Collections*, XXV, 55–57.

I have work cut out for 15 years ahead if the republic and I last so long. . . . .[1]

In *Ancient Society*, which appeared in 1877, Morgan reiterated his analysis of Mexican society in a less combative form. He maintained that what the Spaniards found was not a "kingdom" but simply a confederacy of three Indian tribes—the Aztecs, the Tezcucans, and the Tlacopans—and that the government was administered by a council of chiefs, with the co-operation of a general commander of the military bands. He found indirect evidence in the Spanish writings pointing to both the gens and the phratry, and he interpreted the existence and functions of the council of chiefs and the tenure and functions of the office of the principal war chief all in terms of the Iroquois social organization which he knew so well. To him the Aztec social organization was merely a variant of the general aboriginal American culture pattern, a "military democracy" organized upon *gentes*.[2]

In 1873, Morgan had written an article on Indian architecture in *Johnson's Encyclopedia*, with the purpose of deflating the Munchausenism of the popular accounts of Mexican life as he had done in "Seven Cities of Cibola." Even though he approached all Indian dwellings with the object of interpreting them in terms of the Iroquois "long-house," he was an earnest realist in what he wanted from field workers investigating Mexican ruins.

We want to know the exact nature of the stone of which the former are built, the composition of the mor-

[1] Dated Boston, April 2, 1877.

[2] *Ancient Society*, chap. vii.

tar used; where the stone was obtained and how it was obtained. We want to know how beautiful the "mural paintings" are which are found in these edifices, whether they are Indian daubs or whether they vie with those in the Vatican. We want to know the social organization of the Indians of Mexico and Central America and what they remember of the organization of their ancestors. We want to know whether a relation exists between the plan of the building and the social organization. We know that such a relation exists between the buildings of the Village Indians of New Mexico and their social organization. Possibly, nay probably, the same relation will be found in Mexico and Central America.[1]

With these stringent exactions to investigators, it is little wonder that they preferred to repeat romantic tales of "buried treasures" and other fictions.

In 1878, Morgan visited the Pueblo country with his grandnephews, William Fellowes Morgan and Percy Morgan, and a number of other young men who financed the trip. They took the railroad to Canyon City, the end of the line, and then engaged "a ship of the plain" drawn by a pair of mules and a pair of ponies, and an extra pony. Passing through South Park up to Leadville, which was then booming, due to the discovery of silver, they went south to the Animas and Mancos rivers. There Morgan and others in the party examined some of the ruins. They then passed through the Las Pinos Ute reservation; and from there they journeyed on to Taos, where, with the aid of Spanish interpreters, Morgan attempted to find out the basis of the natives' social organization through an analysis of their kinship

[1] *Rochester Democrat and Chronicle*, July 26, 1881.

terms and also visited the pueblos in the region. After traveling about a thousand miles in six weeks on a wagon the party returned to Canyon City. On the way east, Morgan and William Fellowes Morgan stopped at St. Louis to attend the conference of the American Association for the Advancement of Science, when the former delivered a paper entitled "Observations on the San Juan River District as an Important Seat of Ancient Village Indian Life";[1] and the latter, one on the cave-dwelling of the Mancos.

It was primarily as a result of his interest in the Southwest that Morgan was called upon to present the program for the archaeological expedition into the Pueblo country undertaken by the newly organized Archaeological Institute of America at Harvard. In his report he reiterated his belief that the American aborigines were one common stock, that their institutions, plan of life, usages, and customs were similar; that adaptation to "communism in living" runs through all the house architecture of the Indian tribes; and that this principle determined the form and character of the house itself.[2] Through Morgan's urgent request, Adolph Bandelier went on the expedition; and his reports represent the result of the first extensive exploration of the Southwest. Simultaneously with this investigation was the expedition of M. de Charnay to find "the buried treasures" of Mexico.

[1] Later published in *Peabody Museum of American Archeology and Ethnology, 12th Report*, pp. 536–56.

[2] *Archaeological Institute of America, First Annual Report*, Appendix, pp. 27–80.

Morgan's final treatment of this subject was in *Houses and House Life of the American Aborigines*, which appeared just prior to his death.[1] This monograph contains a résumé of *Ancient Society* and is otherwise merely an expansion of his earlier article in *Johnson's Encyclopedia*. One might consider the following passage of the book his dying message to American ethnologists:

American aboriginal history and ethnology have been perverted and even caricatured in various ways, and among others by a false terminology which itself is able to vitiate the truth. When we have learned to substitute Indian confederacy for Indian kingdom; Teuchtli, or head war chief, sachem and chief for king, prince and lord; Indian villages in the place of "great cities"; communal houses for "palaces" and democratic for monarchic institutions; together with a number of similar substitutions of appropriate for deceptive and improper terms, the Indian of the past and present will be presented understandingly and placed in his true position in the scale of human advancement.[2]

Bandelier, who once characterized Bancroft, in a letter to Morgan, as "the great wholesale book-manufactory at San Francisco who threatens the world with another senseless, brainless compilation," continued the attack on Bancroft after Morgan's death. His polemic zeal brought forth the wrath of Bancroft upon Morgan and his hypotheses. A review in the *Nation* provoked a ranting broadside from Bancroft:

[1] Morgan indicates that this originally formed the fifth part of the manuscript of *Ancient Society*, under the title of "Growth of the Idea of House Architecture."

[2] *Houses and House Life of the American Aborigines*, p. 273.

If I am correctly informed, Mr. Morgan obtained but little information from Mexico and Central America supporting his theory; but as it must be common and universal in order to stand at all, it was necessary his *ipse dixit* should be employed to extend his doctrine over the southern plateau; so with all his strength he said it must be so, and it was so, all eyes and brains to the contrary not-with-standing. . . . . Disciples more wild than their master, have arisen who by the blind pursuit of their *ignis fatuus* are rushing headlong into a gulf of absurdity. . . . . As for the *Nation*, it is regarded by all men as a chronic "sorehead" to please whose writers at all points would be out of the pale of Omnipotence itself. . . . .[1]

Several anthropologists supported Bancroft in the controversy, but Bandelier continued to substantiate Morgan's contentions by citations from Spanish sources and to defend his work vigorously.[2]

Morgan minimized the points of difference between the Aztec and the Iroquois in his dogmatic insistence on the democratic nature of Mexican life. He was too anxious to reduce Montezuma to the level of an Iroquois war chief, and for this reason negated too emphatically many of the Spanish writers whom he was correct in judging generally mendacious. T. T. Waterman, who made a critical examination of the subject, contends that Morgan and Bandelier's positive contributions to Mexican history, especially in regard to the Tenochtitlan, were that they proved that the social organization of this region was based on clans, that the four

[1] *Early American Chroniclers.*
[2] Cf. *The Romantic School of American Archeology.*

phratries and the tribes were loose aggregates of clans held together for the purposes of war and ritual, and that the actions of the tribe as a whole were governed by a council to which the king was responsible.[1] Paul Radin, after an exhaustive analysis of the primary sources, holds that Bandelier was too critical of anything that seemed to credit the ancient Mexicans with a high degree of culture. He concludes that by the time of the Spanish coming, the original democratic nature of the Aztecs had been changed to a caste system based on inequality of distribution of the conquered lands, although he believes that the large landowners had not made serfs of the rest of the tribe. He accepts the statement of the sources also that Montezuma broke with custom and the accepted order of things to change the ruler from an elected chief to a king, a change which he believes was foreshadowed in the elaborate court and the palaces of the chiefs who preceded Montezuma.[2]

Irrespective of the value of Morgan's conclusions on Mexican civilization, his rigid insistence on the necessity for careful and laborious research and field study of the existing Indian groups of the Southwest and archaeological studies of ruins left a permanent impress on American anthropology, and came none too soon in view of the rapid disappearance of these source materials. It was because of his efforts in this direction, that

[1] *University of California Publications in American Archaeology and Ethnology*, XII, 249-82. Cf. John Fiske, *The Discovery of America*, pp. 100-103, 106, 115, 125-30, and also the latter's "The Colonization of the New World" in *The History of All Nations*, Vol. XXI.

[2] *University of California Publications in American Archaeology and Ethnology*, XVII, 1-150.

Professor O. T. Mason declared of Morgan in a letter to him: ". . . . the inductive method of investigating anthropological subjects which you have practiced so successfully entitles you to be placed in the first rank of the School of 'Common Sense' in Anthropology."[1]

[1] Dated Columbian College, Washington, D.C., March 28, 1881.

CHAPTER VI

ANCIENT SOCIETY

I

Ancient Society was Morgan's magnum opus. He revised, summarized, and partially rephrased all his previous ethnological writings and brought them together in this volume. To them he added his general scheme of mankind's progress and applied his idea of the growth of political society to the history of Greece and Rome. It is for the latter reason that the book received the title *Ancient Society*. The subtitle *Researches in the Lines of Human Progress from Savagery through Barbarism to Civilization* indicates that Morgan conceived of the book somewhat in the nature of a history of civilization. However, only twenty-two pages of the almost six hundred page book are devoted to civilizations other than the American Indian and Greek and Roman.

Although the old theological theory of degradation, a corollary of the biblical account of creation, that primitive cultures represented civilizations of men who had "fallen from grace," or, expressed scientifically, were the vestiges of advanced civilizations which had declined, still lingered in some quarters,[1] *Ancient Society* was written at a time when the theory of evolution was in the

[1] See the unsigned review of *Ancient Society* in the *Atheneum*, December 29, 1877, and the discussion of John Lubbock's presidential address before the Royal Anthropological Institute of Great Britain and Ireland in the *Journal* of the Institute, February, 1871, pp. 1-29.

foreground. Morgan's method of approach to his material differed only in detail from that of many writers of his period who were applying the evolutionary methods of the biological and physical sciences to social institutions.

Morgan in his general evolutionary scheme postulates in the manner of Bastian the psychic unity and common origin of mankind, leading to parallel development the world over:

> The history of the human race is one in source, one in experience and one in progress. . . . . Inventions and discoveries show . . . . the unity of origin of mankind, the similarity of human wants in the same stage of advancement, and the uniformity of the operations of the human mind in similar conditions of society.[1]

> . . . . the principal institutions of mankind have been developed from a few primary germs of thought; . . . . the course and manner of their development was predetermined, as well as restricted within narrow limits of divergence by the natural logic of the human mind and the necessary limitations of its powers. Progress has been found to be substantially the same in kind in tribes and nations inhabiting different and even disconnected continents, while in the same status, with deviations from uniformity in particular instances produced by special causes.[2]

> . . . . the experience of mankind has run in nearly uniform channels; human necessities in similar conditions have been substantially the same and the operations of the mental principle have been uniform in virtue

[1] *Ancient Society*, p. vi. The citations are from the Kerr edition, which is most easily available.

[2] *Ibid.*, p. 18.

of the specific identity of the brain of all the races of mankind. . . . .[1]

With one principle of intelligence and one physical form, by virtue of a common origin, the results of human experience have been substantially the same in all times and areas in the same ethnical status. The principle of intelligence although conditioned in its progress within narrow limits of variation, seeks ideal standards invariably the same. Its operations, consequently have been uniform through all the ages of human progress. . . . . A common principle of intelligence meets us in the savage, in the barbarian and in civilized man. It was in virtue of this that mankind was able to produce in similar conditions the same implements and utensils, the same inventions, and to develop similar institutions from the same original germs of thought. . . . .[2]

The influence of contemporary evolutionary geology upon his thinking is seen when he anticipates Tylor in saying:

Like the successive geological formations, the tribes of mankind may be arranged, according to their relative conditions, into successive strata. When thus arranged, they reveal with some degree of certainty the entire range of human progress from savagery to civilization. A thorough study of each successive stratum will develop whatever is special in its culture and characteristics and yield a definite conception of the whole, in their difference and their relations. . . . .[3]

Not satisfied with the Stone, Bronze, and Iron Age classification of the Danish archaeologists, Morgan presented one of his own which was destined to become very

---

[1] *Ibid.*, p. 8.   [2] *Ibid.*, p. 562.

[3] *Ibid.*, p. 506. Cf. E. Tylor, *Journal of Anthropological Institute*, XVIII, 262 *et seq.*

popular. Incorporated in sociological textbooks in America, adopted by Frederick Engels in *The Origin of the Family, Private Property and the State;* and also by John Fiske in his *Discovery of America*, it is still very extensively used. He conceived of mankind the world over passing through or having passed through three successive stages of savagery, barbarism, and civilization, the two earlier of which had a tripartite division of lower, middle, and upper. He recognized that it was "difficult if not impossible to find such tests of progress to mark the commencement of these several periods, as will be found absolute in their application, and without exceptions upon all the continents," and stated that his periods were "provisional." But once having made his arbitrary divisions, he was stubborn and rigid in the application of the "ethnical periods" set forth. The arbitrariness of his divisions may be seen by the fact that a few months before he sent his manuscript to the publisher he had not divided the period of "savagery."[1] Here he divided "savagery" into a "lower status" when man did not know the use of fire and lived on fruits and nuts, and a "middle status" when he acquired a fish subsistence and learned the use of fire. In this group he placed the Australians and the greater part of the Polynesians. In the "upper status of savagery" that came with invention of the bow and arrow, he included the Atapascan tribes of Hudson's Bay Territory, the tribes of the valley of the Columbia, and certain coast tribes

[1] In an address entitled "Ethnical Periods," delivered at the Detroit meeting of the American Association for the Advancement of Science, August, 1875. *Proceedings*, XXIV, 267 *et seq.* The address is chapter i of *Ancient Society* verbatim except for the section dealing with *"Savagery."*

of North and South America. He designated the manufacture of "pottery" as the lower limit of "barbarism." In its "lower status" he placed the Indian tribes of the United States east of the Missouri River and such tribes in Europe and Asia as practiced the art of pottery but were without domesticated animals, which introduced the "middle status of barbarism" in the Eastern hemisphere. Cultivation by irrigation and the use of adobe and stone in architecture began the "middle status of barbarism," in the Western hemisphere and in this category he classified the "Village Indians" of New Mexico, Mexico, Central America, and Peru. The "upper status of barbarism" commenced with the manufacture of iron and ended with the invention of a phonetic alphabet and the use of writing, which ushered in "civilization." He put in this "upper status" the Grecian tribes of the Homeric age, the Italian tribes shortly before the founding of Rome, and the Germanic tribes in the time of Caesar. To the Aryan and Semitic peoples, Morgan ascribes the invention of the phonetic alphabet and adds, "it seems not unlikely the knowledge of iron as well." As could be anticipated, his antecedents were made the initiators of civilization and the "chosen people" of the earth:

In strictness but two families, the Semitic and the Aryan accomplished the work [of attaining civilization] through unassisted self-development. The Aryan family represents the central stream of human progress because it produced the highest type of mankind, and because it has proved its intrinsic superiority by gradually assuming the control of the earth.[1]

[1] *Ancient Society*, p. 562.

This catalogue of cultures is extraordinarily simple, and this simplicity accounts for its wide popularity; but cultures, no matter how primitive, are too complex and the forms of combination of social institutions too variable to fit into any definite social evolutionary scheme. The tenuousness of Morgan's system is revealed even in his presentation. When discussing the groups that belong in the "middle status of barbarism," he included the ancient Britons, "*although familiar with the use of iron*" (italics mine—B. J. S.) which should have placed them in the "upper status." But "the vicinity of more advanced continental tribes had advanced the arts of life among them far beyond the state of development of their domestic institutions."[1] This exposes at once the inherent weakness of any evolutionary classification of culture; all sequences are disturbed by borrowing of cultural traits from neighboring peoples. Morgan recognized this but did not understand its implications when he wrote:

. . . . wherever a continental connection existed, all the tribes must have shared in some measure in each others' progress. All great inventions and discoveries propagate themselves. . . . .[2]

And again:

. . . . some of these inventions were borrowed, not unlikely, from tribes in the Middle Status; for it was by this process constantly repeated that the most advanced tribes lifted up those below them, as fast as the latter were able to appreciate and to appropriate the means of progress.[3]

[1] *Ibid.*, p. 11.   [2] *Ibid.*, p. 39.   [3] *Ibid.*, p. 540.

The cultural and social history of a people can be explained only in the light of its historical relations and cultural contacts, and not by any general universal scheme of evolution. The evolutionary concept put forth by Morgan and others of his period, that human institutions tend to succeed one another in series substantially the same all over the globe, due to "the similarity of human wants" and "the uniformity of the operations of the human mind," must therefore be revised. The peoples of the world have not advanced uniformly in several aspects of culture. The Eskimo has mechanical ingenuity, but his political and social life is crude. The Maya tower above the Negroes in Africa, but their lack of metallurgy puts them lower in Morgan's scale. The difficulty is illustrated by Morgan's error in placing in the very lowest stage the Polynesians, whose culture is among the most complex of the primitive peoples due to their well-developed agriculture and industry; and also the Micronesians, who know textiles and have a fine mythology. In Africa, the bow and arrow was replaced by the more effective spear; and many other groups who have not the bow and arrow are high in other respects, but their status would, irrespective of this fact, be "middle status of savagery." Evolutionary classifications as Morgan's arbitrarily emphasize certain aspects of culture at the expense of others and erroneously postulate a uniform sequence of development failing to recognize the implications of borrowing.

Morgan accounted for the difference in cultural development in the Eastern and Western hemispheres by "the unequal endowments of the continents" but held "the condition of society in the corresponding status must have been in the main, substantially similar."[1] His oft-repeated view explaining the difference between the continents in respect to the primitive domestication of animals on the grounds that in the Western Hemisphere, there was an absence of animals adapted to domestication, excepting the llama, is not valid. The bison of the Great Plains could have been tamed like the buffalo of Southern Asia and the various races of cattle in the Eastern Hemisphere. The caribou, half-tamed by the neighboring Siberian Chukchee and used for food and draft with sledges, could have been used likewise by the Eskimo. Variations in domestication must be explained on cultural grounds, not on geographic.[2]

In the discussion of the "ratio of human progress" Morgan approximates the modern concept of cultural accumulation in a geometric ratio due to the fact that "every item of absolute knowledge gained became a factor in further acquisition, until the present complexity of knowledge was attained." But due to the fact that he did not distinguish between the biological and the cultural, he manifests the naïve belief that

with the production of inventions and discoveries and with the growth of institutions, the human mind necessarily grew and expanded; and we are led to recognize a gradual enlargement of the brain itself, particularly of the cerebral portion.[3] .... We have the same brain, per-

---

[1] *Ibid.*, p. 17. Cf. F. Boas, *XXIe Congrès International des Américanistes* (1924), pp. 21–28.

[2] R. H. Lowie, *Culture and Ethnology*, pp. 47–65. Laurence M. Winters, *Animal Breeding*, p. 171, declares that other animals on this continent were also capable of domestication.

[3] *Ancient Society*, p. 36.

petuated by reproduction, which worked in the skulls of barbarians and savages in by-gone ages; and it has come down to us laden and saturated with the thoughts, aspirations and passions, with which it was busied through the intermediate periods. It is the same brain grown older and larger with the experience of the ages. . . . .[1]

In fact, he called the periods of savagery, barbarism, and civilization "ethnical periods" because he still retained that incredibly fantastic belief discussed previously that

modern institutions plant their roots in the period of barbarism, into which their germs were transmitted from the previous period of savagery. They have had a lineal descent through the ages with the streams of blood, as well as a logical development.[2]

II

Morgan's second evolutionary scheme, as expressed in his section the "Growth of the Idea of Government," has become the classic concept of the political scientists on the origin of the state. Sixteen years previously Henry Maine had made the distinction between government based on kinship affiliation and that based on local contiguity.[3] Morgan goes farther, distinguishing between a gentile society [*societas*], founded upon kinship, which was rooted in a more archaic one based solely on sex, and a political society or state [*civitas*], founded on territory and property. The earliest division based only on sex he discusses vaguely and briefly. It is

[1] *Ibid.*, p. 59.   [2] *Ibid.*, p. 4.

[3] *Ancient Law*, chap. v. Cf. his *Lectures on the Early History of Institutions*, p. 72.

not an essential part of his argument here but is postulated to explain a condition existing among the Kamilaroi where he finds "the sexual and gentile organization both in existence at the same time." Interesting, however, is the fact that he explains Mormonism on this ground:

In the light of these facts some of the excrescences of modern civilization such as Mormonism, are seen to be relics of the old savagism not yet eradicated from the human brain . . . . explainable as a species of mental atavism.[1]

It is to the discussion of the "gentile organization" that he devotes the major part of the book. He finds the gens, phratry, and tribes of the American aborigines analogues of the Grecian gens, phratry, and tribe; the Roman gens, *curia*, and tribe; the Irish sept; the Scottish clan; the Albanian *phrara;* and the Sanskrit *ganas.* He defines the gens as "a body of consanguinei descended from the same common ancestor, distinguished by a gentile name and bound together by affinities of blood," and holds it to be the fundamental basis of government prior to the establishment of the state. He sets forth the characteristics of the Iroquois gens, phratries, and tribes with succinct clarity and then proceeds to interpret in terms of them such institutions among the other American Indian tribes, the Greeks, Romans, and other peoples. He controverts the view of Grote that "the primitive Grecian government is essentially monarchical, reposing on personal feeling and divine right," interpreting the title *basileus* as military commander

[1] *Ancient Society*, p. 59.

rather than king,[1] and insisting that since the government was organized as a gens it *must* have been democratic. His sources on Greece and Rome were Grote, Niebuhr, Maine, Mommsen, and M. de Coulanges, the value of some of whom, Niebuhr especially, had already been questioned by the classical authorities of his period. Morgan placed Theseus and Romulus in the same category as Red Jacket and Corn Planter, and the Roman Senate with the Iroquois Council; but, although he negated differences while looking for likenesses, his fundamental comparison of the classic institutions and those of primitive peoples was epoch-making.

After showing the similarities of those institutions which preceded the state, Morgan's efforts were devoted toward tracing the development of political society based on territory and property from the gentes. He discusses the inauguration of the deme or township by Cleisthenes in Athens in 509 B.C., and holds that from that time forward, the relations of the individual with his gens, which had been based on kinship, were transferred to the township and became territorial and political. He points to similar transition from the *societas* founded upon the gentes to the *civitas* or state founded

[1] Karl Marx commented on this redefinition: "The European scientists, mostly born servants of princes, represent the *basileus* as a monarch in the modern sense. The Yankee republican, Morgan, objects to this. Very ironically but truthfully he says of the oily Gladstone and his *Juventus Mundi:* 'Mr. Gladstone, who presents to his readers the Grecian chiefs of the heroic age as kings and princes, with the superadded qualities of gentlemen, is forced to admit that "on the whole we seem to have the custom or law of primogeniture sufficiently but not oversharply defined." ' As a matter of fact, Mr. Gladstone himself must have perceived that a primogeniture resting on a clause of 'sufficient but not oversharp' definition is as bad as none at all" (F. Engels, *Origin of the Family, Private Property and the State*, p. 127).

upon territory and property in Roman history, and contends that the development of government has everywhere been the same.

Contemporary criticisms of this aspect of Morgan's work were on the whole very favorable. But both Tylor and Lubbock in England insinuated that Morgan had derived his idea of the similarity of the ancient and primitive gens from McLennan without giving him due credit. Lubbock also criticized Morgan for leaving "the Totem and much that it implies out of sight";[1] and Tylor, in his review of the book, sharply objected to Morgan's use of the word "gens."

Students accustomed to precision and consistency like that of Sir Henry Maine in dealing with Ancient institutions cannot but complain of Morgan's treatment of the classic gens. They are at first surprised to find him in his early chapters using the word "gens" and "gentile organization" in writing of the exogamous tribe divisions of the Iroquois and the Australians. Is it not they say, begging the whole question of the origin of the Roman gens to begin by identifying it with the totem clan of the American Indians? On coming to the chapters on the classic gens itself, it is seen that the author tends to justify his use of the word by claiming that "the obligation not to marry in the gens" was held to be the ordinary rule among the Greeks and Romans of the classic period, a novel doctrine which his evidence fails to establish. This position would have been stronger had he been content to argue as McLennan had already done that the classic gens though not distinctly exogamous in historical times, had come out of an earlier exogamous state. . . . .[2]

---

[1] *Saturday Review*, January 5, 1878, pp. 19–21.

[2] *Academy*, July 20, 1878.

The letters of Henry Maine to Morgan reveal with what deep interest he read *Ancient Society* and how he reacted to the theories presented therein:

Many weeks have passed since I received your volume on *Ancient Society*, but I have not acknowledged it simply because I have been reading it very carefully, though slowly, through. Now that I have finished it, I feel that it would be a bad compliment to pass any concise or summary judgment upon it, and I will only say that I have read it with the strongest interest and that there is hardly a chapter which does not present some new material for thought. What opinions I am destined to form on the many new theories which it suggests, I do not know; but I intend to give them that full attention which is deserved by the conscientiousness and laboriousness evident in every part of your work and by the novelty and ingenuity of your inferences. The book cannot fail to make a deep mark on the path of inquiry which we both follow. I have to thank you for the kind mention of my name.[1]

Possibly you may remember that when I thanked you for kindly sending me your work on *Ancient Society*, I told you that I intended to read it with much care. I am now studying it with great attention and with great interest and profit and I have no doubt that I shall have occasion to express myself about it in print. Not indeed that I am likely to trespass on what is strictly your ground. The field of inquiry into the early history of institutions is now so intensive that it may be usefully mapped out into different parts occupying different tendencies. But I have long thought that investigators like yourself who work by actual observation of group customs and those who, like me, are chiefly busy with ancient records and bodies of written law were most

[1] Dated London, July 30, 1877.

likely to find a point of contact in the gens, and hence I am extremely anxious to be sure that I thoroughly understand all your descriptions of the social phenomena to which you attach so much importance.

I need scarcely say that the gens in the early records and law of the higher and more advanced races shows itself at first not only as a self-acting group but as a group occupying a definite local seat. There is also a good deal of evidence that it was a combatant group; part of it is the striking story which I see you notice of the expedition of the Fabii against Veii. All this is perfectly intelligible of the male "gens" i.e. of the gens, theoretically descended from the male and continued through males. In this case, the males who are the muscle of the gens remain in it always and serve for purposes of labour and fighting. I gather from some observations in your 7th Chapter on the "Aztec Confederacy" that you conceive the "male" Indian gentes to have lived together in the same locality; and perhaps you have actually seen this as an existing phenomenon.

But with regard to "female" gentes i.e. gentes believed to have sprung from female and continued through females, I have some difficulty in conceiving them as localised or combatant bodies. It is probable, however, that the difficulty arises solely from my ignorance of facts and hence it comes that I venture to trouble you with some questions about these gentes.

Do the females, through whom alone these gentes are continued remain always in the local seat of the gens, and do their husbands come to them from the seats of other gentes? Do their daughters remain always in the locality and do their sons go abroad to live with wives of other gentes?

Such an organization is quite conceivable and a friend of mine, who has been Chief Justice of the Colony of British Columbia, describes something very like it as prevailing among the Indians of that territory. He describes every male Indian as seeking a wife in some village other than that in which he was born, as going to live with her and as *taking her name*—I presume her gentile name.

But I want to be quite sure of the facts. May I then ask you who are the men of mature age inhabiting the local seat of a "female" gens? I have no doubt that you can answer this in a moment from actual observation and I dare say I could ascertain it in a moment from your "League of Iroquois," but the book does not seem to be procurable in this country.

My hesitation in the matter arises from the difficulty I feel in conceiving a "female" gens, if properly described above as a self-acting or combatant body, since all the men whom one would suppose to be the kernel of the group would be strangers to it by birth.

Could you also tell me to what extent a "female" gens serves as a real check on the intermarriage of real kin. If an Indian has two wives of different "female" gentes, it is surely impossible that their children can intermarry though they are not gentile relatives!

Pardon my troubling you with these questions, in the interest of our subjects which lie so near together.[1]

J. J. McLennan is dangerously ill. I am sorry to say that (as I am told) illness has much increased his acerbity of temper and he is described as employing himself, as well as he can on a book which is to annihilate all his adversaries including myself. If the books which you have sent me suggest any questions which require an answer, I may venture to write you again. Meantime allow me to express the deep interest with which I have read everything you have published, even when on some of the points I do not wholly agree with you.[2]

[1] Dated London, April 30, 1878.

[2] Dated Cambridge, England, November 8, 1880.

Professor J. J. Bachofen, author of the important book *Das Mutterrecht* which influenced Morgan's treatment of the family pronouncedly, acknowledged *Ancient Society* in a manner which revealed his great interest in Morgan's work and also something of the scholar's personality:

Your friendly offer to favour me with a copy of your new work *Ancient Society* reached me this very day. A great admirer of your first important publication on the systems of consanguinity, I did not delay to procure me the foresaid *Ancient Society* some weeks ago from New York with the intention to study the volume in the course of the summer. At the present moment I have only advanced to page fifty, a commencement sufficient to induce me to spare neither time nor labour to overcome the voluminous treatise. I am the more curious to get acquainted with your views on the stages of human progress, as Mr. McLennan's *Studies in Ancient History* London, 1876 seem to me very insufficient in its critical observations, on the ancient systems of consanguinity. Historical inquiries do not admit of being treated as cases in a court of social justice, by reasoning of a barrister. They are mere matter of observation, and the observation of a naturalist, who devotes himself entirely to the facts presented in his microscope. To collect these facts must be the first scope of our endeavorings. I trust the study of your recent publication will considerably enlarge the treasure of such materials destined to serve as building stones for all our systems and personal views. The systems vary and admit of changes according to the progress of the number of facts coming to our knowledge. The materials alone remain and secure to our works a lasting value. In the course of the last years I have devoted much time to extensive reading not without great trouble to procure the works of ancient and modern date, indispensable for the scope I am pursuing. With regard to the ancient American tribes I am still very scarcely provided. The curiosity for that part of mankind would require the aid and friendly assistance of a man so fully acquainted with the literature of the indigenous population of your continent as you show yourself by your numerous writings. The point I am presently taking under special observation, is the relation of brother and sister, brother and nephew or niece by the sister, the question therefore of maternal uncle, the Roman avunculus, so nearly related to the system of exclusive maternal relationship. Any contribution of facts proper to show the distinction of that particular blood-tie among the ancient American tribes would provoke my hearty sympathy. The Indian natives seem to have attached a surprising importance to the relationship of maternal uncle and nephew, and to agree in this respect to the other races of mankind. This particular leads us back to the very origin of our race and accompanies our history through all the stages of advance from savagery, through barbarism to the accomplishment of civilization, but little varying in its meaning and purpose with the development of the family system from its maternal to the unimpaired paternal constitution. If you allow me to point out a special work, I met with in numerous quotations, I would refer to your history of the League of Iroquois. Another source of high interest must be the materials collected by the State Inquiries into the Indian affairs, but above all the proper traditions, myths, songs of the Indians themselves, as far as they have been collected by the care of modern students. . . . .[1]

After having studied your work on *Ancient Society* from beginning to end, I cannot withhold from expressing to its author my best gratitude for all the valuable

[1] Dated Basle, May 14, 1878.

contributions to a systematical knowledge of the subject it treats, a subject so intimately connected with my own researches. The investigations of the systems of consanguinity and affinity especially with regard to the North American Indians together with the work now in question will become the starting point of a series of investigations, full of new perspective into a period of human existence hitherto scarcely taken notice of. The light thrown now on a multitude of facts contained in the traditions of the ancient European classical world not only confirms the views contained in my own book on M. R., but favors in a very great measure the discovery of a very considerable mass of single remnants of the barbarian period preserved in ages of a quite different turn of mind and of the highest stage of ancient civilization. Passages that formerly did not awaken any notice, now arrest our attention and become intelligible. .... *Verbum non amplius ad.*[1]

His long letter to Morgan on the origin and nature of the Roman gens indicates the status of pre-Roman history in his day:

.... The question you touch in your last letter, the origin and nature of the Roman gens, is one of vast research and still unsettled in spite of all efforts made to bring it to its solution. The light thrown on the subject by the classical authorities is but an accidental one and wholly insufficient to clear up the different faces it brings before us. What we know with perfect safety consists in 3 characteristics, *videlicet* 1. that the gens belonged exclusively to the patricians. 2. that it was in the exclusive possession of the *auspicea* and therefore distinguished by a religious character, that prevented its being ever suppressed by any change in the form of government. 3. that it was intimately connected with the sys-

[1] Dated Basle, November 21, 1878.

tem of paternity in monogamous marriage of patricians *inter se* exclusively. Intermarriage between the different gentes appears to have been allowed from the beginning without having been enforced by law. The *gentis enuptio* as a privilege seems to be restricted to the category of the libertie and may be taken as a remnant of a system of community which in historical times has ceased to govern the gentile organization. Now of the 3 characteristics enumerated the religious one is the most prominent and the most urged upon by the Roman historians. The sacred character of the gens and consequently of the patricians in common constitutes true distinctif of that portion of the Roman community by contraposition to the plebian bulk of the Quirites, and forms the groundwork on which the very existence of Rome as a political body is built. Down to the times of Imperial Rome, the *gentes patricice* formed the chain which fettered the state to its heavenly authors and protectors who refused to communicate with anyone but the patricians, the exclusive organs of their will and instructions. Here we see that the Roman gentes take the importance of a political institution from the very first day of the formation of the city, and that consequently we find ourselves far removed from the natural growth of these unities of blood relations. This is not impossible and has often been regarded as a probable supposition, that from the beginning the gentes have been an artificial agglomeration of families not related by blood ties and that by neglecting cognation the author of the Roman state has only been enabled to give to his organization the symmetry and equilibrium, that blood unities, when strictly required, would not have allowed to obtain in the same measure. I do not venture to decide so heavy a question: but at all events the natural history of the gentes is to be sought in the pre-Roman period, the political organization putting an end to the clanships of barbarian nations. Here lies the fundamental difference between the Romans and the American Indians, with whom a corresponding degree of political advancement never has shown itself, not even with the Iroquois confederacy, the most advanced among them. Hence the very extreme caution we must use in comparing the two peoples, Romans and Iroquois. We never ought to forget that the Romans never have been a nation but a political body, that they owe their very existence to the negation of what makes and constitutes a nationality founded on common origin and finally from beginning to end one idea only, the idea of a political state, governed the brain of all citizens. Take the tradition of the victorious Horatius slaying his sister mourning the loss of her beloved. Does it not *quasi* embody the principle of all human history, *videlicet*, that all natural feeling, all claims of the most revered bloodtie, have no right when in contradiction with the idea of political advancement? The *sororium tigillum* as a sacred emblem marks the boundary of a bygone age. The nation of Quirites is changed into a populus Romanus Quiritium. By the same process the principle of maternal descent is put aside. It belongs to the pre-Roman period, the natural point of view no more being taken in consideration. I am perfectly aware what remnants of the ancient zoölogical principles are to be found in the oldest traditions, that the Sylvia gens of Alba Longa was a maternal one, that in the history of the Roman kings the succession of the female line was not yet set aside, that the wide reaching crime of Parricidium admits of no other explanation that by means of maternity combined with a family institution not yet very far from bride promiscuity: but what I cannot oversee at the same time is the decided opposition formed by Rome against the prevalence of this law of former existence. Nothing can be more clearly established than the maternal principle of the Sabine family. Rome took the Sabine virgins, received Sabine clans in its community, but rejected their maternal principle as inconsistent with its political idea. The same may be said of the Etruscans. The sister's son of the last Tarquinius found no grace at Rome. The Favia gens, evidently of Etruscan connection, throw aside their maternal principle, retaining at Rome but one vestige of her former law, the prenomen Numerius. Egypt in later times opposed the predominance of maternity to the Roman principle of paternity, that the Roman lawyer in his responsum asserted as the only admissible in the Roman empire. More examples of the same struggle might be advanced: but those put down show sufficiently what I insist upon: *videlicet* the pre-Roman period as the very seat of the first steps of the Italian nations towards the development of what we call the natural gens. Hence arises the difficulty of arriving at a settled opinion on the question, what the Italian gens originally may have been; the classical sources are insufficient to bring us to a result more than hypothetical. That period of human existence must be studied by the observations of nations still existing, as you have done in so instructive a manner and with so brilliant success. For me, I do not venture any criticism on your chapter on the Roman gens. A very minute study of the question ought to precede any attempt in that direction. The question is of too great an importance to be lost sight of. But time is required to ponderate the argument you lay down in your work and to measure them with those advanced by Mr. Tylor in the Academy and Mr. Girand Teulon in his treatise "La famille." I hope to enable myself to detail more profusely on this subject in future letters. . . . .[1]

Bachofen dedicated a book to Morgan in appreciation of his work:

[1] Dated Basle, January 24, 1879.

Today I have mailed two volumes of small essays, one for yourself and one for the Smithsonian Institution of Washington. The subjects discussed stand in close connection with the *Mutterrecht* and accordingly give me a desired opportunity through dedication of the book to express my thanks to you publicly for the extensive information given me by your writings and for your interest in my own endeavors. The fundamental point of view is the same as you expressed in your last communication: I place the phenomena of the so-called classical antiquity in parallel with other corresponding phenomena whether of decayed people of civilization or of still existing barbarian races; and endeavor through these last to explain and render understandable whatever that is seen in the former that is obscure. I intend to extend this procedure much further than is done in these first thirty numbers and in this way to arrive at the discussion of the Roman gentes. I am entirely convinced that the correspondence of the Iroquois (to choose this tribe as illustration) to the Roman tribes, as well in their inner disposition as in the principle of confederation, is a complete one and that only in the way of comparative investigation can one attain to further insight and to true understanding. The German scholars especially the philologists of the classical nations, are troubled with a pitiable one-sidedness. Seldom does their vision go beyond the narrow limits of the ancient world, yea over those of its separate nations. All is first isolated, torn from every connection and then in accordance with modern ideas of practise, judged, criticised and at last completely bungled. This is connected with the German smoke filled study rooms and also with the narrow political relations of the German people, whose vision is not accustomed to any breadth. . . . . Roman and Greeks pass as select who should never be compared with barbarian tribes. They could learn from barbarian tribes. . . . .[1]

[1] Dated Basle, October 28, 1880.

.... German scholars propose to make antiquity intelligent by measuring it according to our popular ideas of our own present. They only see themselves as creations of the past. Hence stupidity, to reject all traditions that will not allow to be treated that way. . . . . The final result of such vanity is nothing else but a deplorable misrepresentation of the beginning of human growth, resembling the pictures of the past century, that represent Coriolanus in the attire of a life guard of Louis XIV and Veturia in the dressing of the dame of honour at a court festival. What has been made of Coriolanus? A puerile nurse story that ought not to be taken notice of by serious brain. It seems to me the same case with the gentes and the Roman kings. Prototypes they become of the Roman Emperor and the poor aristocracy that narrowed his throne. . . . . You see that I agree with some of your fundamental ideas perfectly. But at the same time I confess that great difficulties remain that cannot be overcome by the sole principle of gentilism as established in your work. If we had only to do with the indigenous population of Italy, the task would be very simplified, the parallelism with your Indian tribes a totally corresponding one. But many colonists settled there. . . . . I conclude: gentilism with all its surrounding combinations is a great groundwork of Roman history, but not the only one . . . . its undisputed existence is to be traced to a period anterior to any historical condition. It never has lost its value.[1]

The distinction between gentile and political society established by Maine and Morgan is still held as valid by modern anthropologists in so far as conceptually a union of kinsmen differs from a union of neighbors and in so far as the blood tie·is often the dominant element in governmental activities of primitive societies. Lowie

[1] Dated Basle, January 4, 1881.

contends, however, that although kinship relationship is the dominant factor, the territorial factor is always functioning, even in the most primitive groups. Local territorial ties and kinship ties coexist among all peoples, kinship involving one set of obligations, territorial relations another. The basic problem is not that of explaining how suddenly a change was effected from government by kinship affiliation to one by territorial contiguity, for both are always present, but to show what processes strengthened the emphasis on territory.[1] Manifestations of extreme jealousy regarding territorial rights have been noted among primitive peoples; in fact, Morgan himself ascribes as the first characteristic of the tribe the possession of a territory.[2] There are in primitive society also various "associations," such as men's clubs, age classes, and secret organizations, which function independently of kinship relationship, which Morgan neglects entirely in his discussion.[3] Lowie originally ascribed to the latter the disrupting force in the transition from kinship affiliation to the strengthening of the local tie in the form of the political state, but later he substantially modified this position.[4] Malinowski's treatment of the concept of fatherhood among the Trobriand Islanders gives a new slant to the discussion in indicating that kinship may itself be derivative of the local territorial factor, that there is there a spatial de-

[1] *Origin of the State*, pp. 52 et seq., 72.

[2] *Ancient Society*, p. 113.

[3] H. Cunow, *Die Verwandtschafts-Organisation in der Australneger*, pp. 25 et seq., 144 et seq.; H. Schurtz, *Altersklassen und Männerbunde*, pp. 1–82.

[4] *Primitive Society*, pp. 257–96; *Freeman*, V, 440–42, 465–67; *Origin of the State*, pp. 75, 93, 101.

terminant underlying the sentiments involved in kinship relationships.[1]

The problem of the origin of the state is a much more complex one than Morgan indicated, but his basic distinctions still apply with the important modifications suggested. In view of Morgan's popularity in socialist circles, it is important to note that he never grasped the significance of the modern state as a class institution. Not only did he fail to approximate the Marxian formulation of the state as an organ of class domination, refined by Lenin,[2] but he also did not sense the importance of caste as a precursor of the state, as Gumplowicz[3] and Oppenheimer[4] have done.

III

The preconceptions underlying Morgan's scheme of the evolution of the family are characteristic of his period. He thought of monogamy: "The whole previous experience and progress of mankind culminated and crystallized in this pre-eminent institution,"[5] the realization of which "the selfishness of mankind as distinguished from womankind, delayed . . . . until that great fermentation of the human mind which ushered in civilization."[6] He likewise, following the fashion of his day, conceived of stages leading up to monogamy, which

[1] *Father in Primitive Psychology*, pp. 11–18, 86–94. Cf. his *Sex and Repression in Savage Society*.

[2] *State and Revolution*.

[3] *Der Rassenkampf*. Cf. W. G. Sumner and A. Keller, *Science of Society*, Vol. I, chaps. xvii–xviii.

[4] *The State*.   [5] *Ancient Society*, p. 512.

[6] *Ibid.*, p. 470. Cf. J. J. Bachofen, *Das Mutterrecht*.

"alone was able to place societies on a moral basis." He repeated the sequences formulated in *Systems of Consanguinity*, changing the pedantic terminology without simplifying it, and distinguished five successive forms of the family preceded by promiscuity. The first family was the "consanguine family," in which there existed an intermarriage of brothers and sisters. The second the "punaluan family," tending to check the intermarriage of brothers and sisters, which was the basis of the organization into gentes excluding brothers and sisters from the marriage relation. The third was the "syndyasmian family," which was "marriage between single pairs but without exclusive cohabitation;" the fourth, in a limited area among pastoral people, the "patriarchal family," founded on the marriage of one man with several wives; and fifth, the "monogamian," coming with the rise of property and the settlement of lineal succession to estates and involving exclusive cohabitation. He regarded the first, second, and fifth as important and existing, and the third and fourth as intermediate forms and not "influential." The types of the family were "not separated from each other by sharply defined lines" but by "insensible gradations . . . . they have sprung successively from one another and they represent collectively the growth of the idea of the family."[1]

When Morgan was writing *Systems of Consanguinity*, he found it difficult to explain the origin of the classificatory system. He adopted the suggestion of his friend, the Rev. J. H. McIlvaine, that it arose from the Hawaii-

---

[1] *Ancient Society*, pp. 394–95.

an system or "punaluan" family, which they considered most primitive because it was most obnoxious to them.[1] Judge Lorin Andrews had written to Morgan that under such a system ". . . . two or more brothers with their wives, or two or more sisters with their husbands, were inclined to possess each other in common."[2] Morgan argued that such a family must have been a "reformatory" movement from a previous stage when brothers and sisters intermarried, i.e., the "consanguine family":

The existence of the Consanguine family must be proved by other evidence than the production of the family itself. As the first and most ancient form of the institution, it has ceased to exist even among the lowest tribes of savages. It belongs to a condition of society out of which the least advanced portion of the human race have emerged. . . . . Proof is found in a system of consanguinity and affinity . . . . which remains to attest the fàct that such a family existed when the system was formed. That system is the Malayan. It defines the relationships that would exist in a consanguine family and *it demands the existence of such a family to account for its own existence* [Italics mine.—B. J. S.].[3]

Proof of the previous existence of the "consanguine family" is, therefore, solely a logical one derived from Morgan's interpretation of the "Malayan" (Hawaiian) kinship system which he felt could only be understood by postulating the earlier intermarriage of brother and sister.

The "consanguine family" also must have been an improvement of a previous condition, he argued:

[1] *Systems of Consanguinity*, p. 479.
[2] *Ancient Society*, p. 436.   [3] *Ibid.*, p. 410.

Finally, it will be perceived that a state of society indicated by the consanguine family points with logical
directness to an anterior condition of promiscuous intercourse. There seems to be no escape from this conclusion
though questioned by so eminent a writer as Mr. Darwin. . . . . The most that can safely be claimed upon
this difficult question is, that the consanguine family
was the first organized form of society and that it was
necessarily an improvement upon the previous unorganized state, whatever that state may have been. It
found mankind at the bottom of the scale from which as
a starting point, and the lowest known we may take up
the history of human progress and trace it through the
growth of domestic institutions, inventions and discoveries, from savagery to civilization. . . . . With the
existence of the consanguine family established, of
which the proofs adduced seem to be sufficient, the remaining families are easily demonstrated.[1]

Again later, in summary, he wrote:

. . . . the consanguine family and the Malayan system
of consanguinity presuppose antecedent promiscuity
. . . . the consanguine family is stamped with the marks
of this supposed antecedent state. It is recognized promiscuity within defined limits, and those not the nar-
rowest, and it points through its organism to a worse
condition against which it interposed a shield. . . . .
Promiscuity may be deduced theoretically as a necessary condition antecedent to the consanguine family;
but it lies concealed in the misty antiquity of mankind
beyond the reach of positive knowledge. . . . .[2]

[1] *Ibid.*, p. 427.

[2] *Ibid.*, pp. 507–9. Lubbock became sarcastic when confronted with such
naïve arguments: ". . . . Mr. Morgan's sort of logic is exposed in all its
originality. Brothers and sisters must have intermarried and that knowingly,
and with the solemnity of an institution because if they did not, Mr. Morgan

In brief, Morgan's concept of the growth of the family logically required the existence of the "consanguine family," which in turn logically required an unorganized state or promiscuity to complete the proof of evolution from the lowest to the highest form: "This system of relationship, instead of revolting the mind, discloses with sensible clearness, 'the hole of the pit whence [we have been] digged' by the good providence of God."[1] He offers no proof of promiscuity other than to say, when discussing it: ".... the lessening volume of the skull and its increasing animal characteristics as we recede from civilized to savage man, deliver some testimony concerning the necessary inferiority of primitive man."[2]

He likewise considers that the fact that one of the Herods was married to his sister, and Cleopatra was married to her brother, as "much more satisfactorily explained as the remains, as well as the evidence of an ancient custom than as a lapsed condition of private morals."[3]

Controversies over Morgan's scheme of the evolution of family have been extensive and acrimonious. The first aspect of the controversy was concerned with the question of the reality of a previous stage of promiscuity, which had likewise been postulated by Lubbock,[4] McLennan,[5] and Bachofen.[6] Darwin set the pattern of later critics of this position by contending that promis-

---

cannot explain the reason of the Malayan system of calling aunts mothers, nephews sons, and the rest of it" (*Saturday Review*, January 5, 1878).

[1] *Systems of Consanguinity*, p. vi.   [4] *Origin of Civilisation*, chap. iii.

[2] *Ancient Society*, p. 507.   [5] *Primitive Marriage*, p. 163.

[3] *Systems of Consanguinity*, p. 480.   [6] *Das Mutterrecht, passim.*

cuity among mankind was unlikely since anthropoid apes were not promiscuous and that aboriginal man "probably lived in small communities, each with a single wife, or if powerful with several, whom he jealously guarded against all other men."[1] Westermarck's arguments against primitive promiscuity have been recently challenged by Briffault on the grounds that the earlier accounts of the mating habits of anthropoid apes are unreliable and that ethnological evidence is in favor of promiscuity.[2] The outcome of the controversy over whether promiscuity has ever been discovered among existing primitive peoples does not affect Morgan's thesis here, for he was of the opinion that promiscuity and the "consanguine family" belonged "to a condition of society out of which the least advanced portion of the human race has emerged."

Morgan sought support for his views on "consanguine marriage" and a previous condition of promiscuity from Lorimer Fison, the Australian anthropologist, with whom he was in constant correspondence and for whose entrance into anthropology he was responsible.[3] Fison's letters on these points are very revealing:

[1] *Descent of Man*, chap. xx.

[2] E. Westermarck, *History of Human Marriage* (5th ed.), I, 103–336; *ibid.*, III, 223–66; R. Briffault, *Mothers*, I, 614–781; *ibid.*, II, 2–96. Both volumes contain extensive bibliographies on the controversy. The books listed therein have been consulted in the preparation of this volume, but are not noted among the selected references.

[3] For evidence of the great influence of Lewis Henry Morgan on Australian anthropology, cf. "Selections from the Letters of Lorimer Fison and A. W. Howitt to Lewis Henry Morgan," edited by the author, *American Anthropologist*, N.S., XXXII, 257–79, 419–53.

. . . . With regard to the Consanguine family, I accept it theoretically as presenting the only reasonable solution of the terms of kinship such as those of Hawaii Rotuma etc. All I say with regard to it as a stepping point is precisely what you say yourself—that no tribe has been found with it in present existence. The traces of its former prevalence appear to me to be clear and unmistakable, but I cannot say of it what we can say of the exogamous intermarrying classes, simply because we can find the latter still prevailing. You must take into account the fact that my position indicates extreme caution in my statements. I should shock and grieve many of my best friends whom I should be very sorry to offend, and who might easily be offended on such a matter. Some of our old fashioned ministers for instance. Hence while I do not feel at liberty to exercise a reticence which would be cowardly and dishonest, I feel constrained to exercise the very greatest caution in my statement. My own opinion is that the former existence of the Consanguine family is proved by the evidence but I do not assert this. I point out that the evidence *seems* to establish it; but that as we can find no present instance of it in actual existence, we need not go any further back than the Divided Commune while investigating the present gentile arrangements and comparing them with those recorded in history. I hope this will be sufficiently clear from my book. My statement is in brief—The evidence points strongly to a former Undivided Commune. Granted this and from your "reformatory movement" all the rest flows. This seems to me to be a strong argument for the old Undivided Commune, but I have carefully guarded myself against a *positive assertion* that it existed. Moreover I am not satisfied in my own mind that the matrimonial right was ever exercised habitually to its full extent. The right existed and was acknowledged. It is the one fundamental fact underlying the whole system of relationship. But it seems probable that its actual assertion in the individual cases would soon become restricted more or less. This however does not in any way affect the main theory. The right is fully established and its general exercise is still apparent on occasions. Only by last mail, Howitt sent me an account of an Australian tribe non-Kamilaroi who betroth their girls in infancy. When the "husband" considers the girl is of sufficient age, he goes after her into the forest with his friends and seizes her. Not he but his friend consummates the marriage. The girl is common for some days to all his tribal brothers and not until they have all exercised their right, does his own come into force. But henceforth it is paramount. This is a very striking instance of expiation for marriage. I have fully satisfied myself by inquiries in Fiji that infant betrothal is a protection against the old communal right. This we shall set forth in a special article as soon as possible. . . . .[1]

I have been thinking over what I said to you about the Consanguine Family etc. and it occurs to me that I may as well say a little more. From your own remarks I am afraid that my words have been taken by you and may perhaps be taken by others to mean more than I meant by them. For my own part it seems clear to me that we need not go beyond the exogamous clans or clan for an explanation of all the later developments up to and far on this side of the Roman gens, provided always that we recognise the vast importance of the descent from females to males. This is the work toward which I have set my face and everything which is beyond its outer line is unnecessary to my purpose. . . . . When I say that to the point where I stop "is far enough for us to go" I mean that it is far enough for my own purposes. The road beyond is extremely tempting. It shows itself

[1] Dated Navuloa, Fiji, October 1, 1880.

clearly to me and looks like a solid road. To my own mind the proofs of its existence are such that nothing but its existence (i.e. its former existence) can account for the facts. But we cannot find a present instance of it. Its use has passed away from the earth as you yourself affirm: the task I propose to myself is to trace the steps in the formation of the gens from the present usage of savage tribes, and therefore what is beyond that present usage is foreign to my purpose. Even this however, requires explanation and great qualification, because in point of fact I do go beyond present usage, and I had to guard myself against positive assertion of the former existence of the Undivided Commune. As it is, several passages in Kamilaroi and Kurnai appear to take it for granted. In my own mind I accept it as sufficiently proved, but I do not positively assert it for these two reasons:

1. I expect violent opposition and therefore resolved to narrow as far as possible the ground of controversy.

2. The Undivided Commune means nothing more nor less than "promiscuity" and this would be terribly shocking to many of my best friends among our ministers. They would suppose it to involve conclusions which do not appear to me to be involved, and no argument of mine would avail to persuade them that the theory is not subversive of "the faith." As it is, I have had some little trouble and expect more. . . . . If at any time we can find a tribe of savages living in the condition to which the evidence points, then I shall be constrained to go farther myself and to *assert* that which I now admit only a strong probability. I admit this probability in my book and in my own mind I admit more than a probability. In short I do not doubt the former existence of the Undivided Commune but I do not consider it as necessary to my purpose to assert it and moreover (owing to my surroundings) it were better for me not to assert it as long as assertion is unnecessary.

. . . . You say "If you believe the Consanguine Family to be the necessary deduction from the Polynesian system, I shall feel greatly assured." I have no hesitation in saying that I do consider it, because in no other way can I account for that system. The *theory* of marriage among savages appears to me to be clearly based upon the fundamental notion that the *Individual*—the Social Unit—is a group of Individuals. Hence flows logically the entire system of relationship and descent. And the constitution of that group is determined by the terms of relationship. As I say in my chapter on Group Mar. and Rel. "The terms of kinship now in everyday use point out the groups and the groups taken as units explain the *raison d'être* of the terms." But for the special purpose of my work I do not consider it necessary to go beyond the division of the group into exogamous groups such as we find in the present day. Purposely, as far as I am concerned, I have narrowed the controversy to this ground. Thus I have taken up as it were an advanced post which seems to me impregnable and which covers the country behind it. If it can be maintained, we may defy the enemy's attempts to get behind it.

. . . . "Unattached" in savage society, at least where the clan organization has not been broken up, a man cannot exist without some sort of connection with some clan or other. In Fiji, where we have a distinct god-born class of chiefs, or nobles, broken men frequently attach themselves to a chief and are very useful to him. They have no status in his clan. Hence they are anxious to distinguish themselves by usefulness in peace and by bravery in war, for thus only can they earn the right to exist. Hence arises the practice of Commendation. A broken man must attach himself to somebody or he perishes. A Noman's man is like a barnacle which misses its way and finds nothing to adhere to. There is no possibility of independent existence. . . . .[1]

[1] Dated Navuloa, Fiji, October 7, 1880.

It was Morgan's view that the gens arose as "a reformatory movement" initiated by primitive peoples to prevent the intermarriage of real kin, a view which Lorimer Fison and A. W. Howitt,[1] Baldwin Spencer,[2] and later Frazer supported.[3] After the sharp criticism of McLennan and Lubbock, the former of whom declared that Morgan's solution of the origin of the family "failing to explain the phenomena must sink below the level of reasonable guessing,"[4] Morgan attempted to clarify his views in his Preface to Fison and Howitt's *Kamilaroi and Kurnai*, concluding: ". . . . it is not supposable that savages design consciously, reformatory movements in the strict sense." His whole theory, however, is dependent upon the assumption that the various changes were designed reforms (it is difficult to understand what is implied by "unconscious reforms"), and *Systems of Consanguinity* and *Ancient Society* are permeated with this belief. The unsatisfactory nature of his hypothesis of the origin of the gens by a "reformatory movement" reinforced by natural selection has been thoroughly exposed by Morgan's critics. Lubbock wrote:

. . . . all Mr. Morgan's theory of the gens as constructed by various reforms and restrictions, imposed for moral and sanitary reasons on Punaluan and Consanguine marriages, may be regarded as being built on

[1] *Kamilaroi and Kurnai.* Cf. A. W. Howitt, *Journal of the Anthropological Institute,* XII, 499–504.

[2] *Transactions of the Australasian Association for the Advancement of Science, 1904,* pp. 419 *et seq.*

[3] *Totemism and Exogamy,* I, 285 *et seq;* IV, 107.

[4] *Studies in Ancient History* (1st ed.), p. 371. Cf. Lubbock, *Nature,* December 14, 1876.

sand. There is no evidence at all for any such formal and widely prevalent institutions as those on which Mr. Morgan erects his theory. Even if there were, it is impossible to understand how the lowest savages came to "perceive the evils" of their institutions. Moral objections they could not urge *ex hypothesi* and sanitary objections do not dawn quite so early on minds which by the argument, are purblind.[1]

It is yet a question whether inbreeding is biologically detrimental to the race. Furthermore, the gens cannot be regarded as a device to prevent inbreeding, affecting as it does only one-half of the field of consanguinity, and permitting marriage among close relatives.[2]

Morgan was especially unfortunate in accepting McIlvaine's suggestion that the gens was a "reformatory movement" from the Polynesian (Hawaiian) system. For, as indicated previously, the Polynesian culture was an advanced one, not that of a group that could be placed at the lowest of the scale and from which the gens had developed. Further researches by Cunow and Rivers have revealed distinct kinship terms among these people, not noted by Morgan, for "brother-in-law" and "sister-in-law" and other nomenclature which indicate that it cannot possibly be a development from a "consanguine family" but is instead a late development.[3]

[1] *Saturday Review*, January 5, 1878, p. 20. Cf. N. Thomas, *Kinship Organisation and Group Marriage in Australia*, pp. 111 *et seq.*

[2] H. J. Spinden, "Formal Inbreeding in Human Society," *Eugenics, Genetics and the Family*, pp. 288 *et seq.*

[3] H. Cunow, *op. cit.*, pp. 54, 127 *et seq.;* cf. his *Zur Urgeschichte der Ehe und Familie*, pp. 50 *et seq.* Cunow was otherwise very sympathetic to Morgan's view. W. H. R. Rivers, *Anthropological Papers Presented to E. B. Tylor*, pp. 317 *et seq.*

Horatio Hale criticized Morgan along this line in his frank letter commenting on *Ancient Society:*

I have only recently had the opportunity of perusing your excellent work on *Ancient Society*. Being in New York a few weeks ago, I obtained a copy from the publisher, and have read it with the careful attention it well deserves, and, I may add with great interest and instruction. Your account of the gens appears to me particularly admirable. One could hardly have supposed that the organization of the tribe of American Indians could be so studied and analyzed, as to throw a new and vivid light on the early history of Greece and Rome. It seems to me, however, that you have done this, and that your work will hereafter rank with Niebuhr's, as initiating a new era and method in the treatment of ancient history. I was glad to learn at the publishers that your volume has sold well in England, where—as well as in Germany and France—its merits are likely to be appreciated.

You will hardly expect that your views on the "ancient family" (in your Part III) will meet with the same general acceptance as those relating to government and property. The latter do not seem to me to depend at all upon the former. The gens might arise as readily in a monogamic population as in any other. I must frankly say that man has always been a "pairing animal." I cannot persuade myself that he began his social life in promiscuous intercourse, far below most of the brutes and only by slow degrees and after ages of progress attained to the level of the tiger, the swallow, and the chimpanzee. It seems to me that this inclination to pair is a natural instinct, similar to paternal affection, and entirely distinct from men's sexual desire. I doubt if the marriage of brothers and sisters has at any time been common. It would contravene another law of human nature, or principle, which makes the growth of sexual desire between individuals of different sexes who live much together very unusual and all but impossible. This law affects according to my observation, not only parents and children, brothers and sisters, but also non-related persons who reside together. It is owing to this law that the "co-education of the sexes" has been found to be so safe to the surprise of many persons who imagined that the two sexes were like spark and tinder. I think I have seen the influence of this law among the lower animals. And I believe it to be the law which in communal households, has given rise to the custom "of exogamous marriages."

Your researches into the history of relationships which prevail among different races appear to me very interesting and valuable. The deductions, however, which I draw from them are different from those which you so ably set forth. I look upon the "classificatory system" as the necessary outgrowth of the "communal household," where a number of nearly related families dwell under the same roof, their children forming one company or flock, between all of whom and all the grown people there is a natural and, so to speak, an undiscriminatory affection. It is easy to see how this mode of speech would then arise. I am, we will suppose, a married Hawaiian, living in a large house along with my married brothers and perhaps my married sisters and cousins. The little children who play about me when I am at work in my field or who go out fishing with me in my canoe are all alike dear to me. When I speak of or to them, I don't use the words "son" or "daughter," "niece" or "nephew." I classify them. I may add the words "male" or "female" for further distinction. In like manner I am not in their speech a father or uncle. I am an "old one" a "senior" and if necessary they may distinguish the sex in like manner. Among themselves, the children have no word exactly equivalent to "brother" or "sister" or "cousin." They have expressions which mean "mate" or "comrade" and they may further distinguish by adding words or using forms to indicate whether the mate is male or female, or whether older or younger than the speaker. All this is classificatory, and it is pure Hawaiian. "Keiki" is not "child" but "little one." It is a compound of "Kahi" (contracted to "ke") and "iki" "little"—the adjectives in Hawaiian always following the nouns. "Makua" means "old," or "mature." It is applied to trees and fruit as much as to human beings. "Makua kani" and "makuna wahini" mean simply "male elder" (or grown person) and "female elder." The entire list of relationships may be analysed in the same manner. I may speak with some positiveness on these points having studied the language carefully in preparing my comparative grammar and Lexicon of the Polynesian dialects.

The lists of relationships which you have collected with so much industry and care seem to me to prove not that brothers and sisters were accustomed to marry nor yet that brothers and sisters had their wives and husbands in common but simply and solely that in the early history of most races it has been customary for nearly related families to live together in large households, for mutual support and protection. This is an interesting fact and particularly valuable as showing how the gens probably originated. I cannot but think that in attempting to strain the significance of the terms of relationship further than this, you have formed theories which contravene the laws of human nature, and you have actually done injustice to the value of your researches.

I know that you will deem the frank expression of my views the best compliment which I can pay to the excellence of your work. If I had not been so profoundly impressed with its value, I should not have thought worth while to point out the few portions which seem to me to need reconsideration. . . . .[1]

Intimately related with Morgan's discussion of the evolution of the family are his judgments concerning the original universality of the gens, the priority of the maternal gens or clan over the paternal, the relation of the gens to the family, and the meaning and implications of kinship terms—all of which have been sources of animated controversy. Morgan believed that the gens was universal in aboriginal America; but when Swanton[2] points out that it was not found among the existing Salish, Athapascan, and Eskimo groups, he is merely corroborating what Morgan had admitted. Morgan ventured explanations for this absence by asserting that the Eskimos' occupation of the American continent was recent and that they did not belong to the American Indian family. In regard to the Salish and Athapascan groups, he contended that since the Columbia valley was the "nursery land of the Ganowanian family" and the initial point of its migrations, "it seems probable that their ancestors possessed the organization into gentes, and that it fell in decay and finally disappeared."[3] That the gens was never universal, even in America, is now certain. The great variability of the *sibs* (Morgan's gens) has led Lowie to claim several independent centers of *sib* diffusion in North America, a view which has not had wide acceptance.[4]

[1] Dated Clinton, Ontario, December 30, 1878.

[2] *American Anthropologist*, N.S., VII, 662–73. Cf .C. Wissler, *Introduction to Social Anthropology*, pp. 159–82.

[3] *Ancient Society*, pp. 181–82.   [4] *American Journal of Sociology*, XX, 91.

Morgan, under the influence of Bachofen's *Das Mutterrecht*,[1] and by his interpretation of the status of women among the Iroquois, had contended, as had McLennan, that maternal descent universally preceded paternal descent. Swanton,[2] Lowie,[3] Kroeber,[4] and Goldenweiser[5] have been instrumental in controverting this view which Tylor,[6] Frazer,[7] and more recently Hartland[8] have supported. In this field more than in any other, primitive Australia has contributed data to support evolutionism and primitive America has fostered anti-evolutionary views. The classical evolutionists bring evidence from Australia to prove the priority of matrilineal type of organization by showing that it exists among the most primitive tribes while the most advanced tribes are among those with patrilineal descent. The American ethnologists counter that, granted that this is true in Australia, it is not universally true, for in America the opposite situation existed. In the three areas in America where unilateral descent prevailed, both matrilineal and patrilineal groups are found; and in each case the groups with the richest culture are

[1] Morgan acknowledges this influence (*Ancient Society*, p. 359).

[2] Swanton *op. cit.*, p. 670. Cf. his article in *Anthropos*, IX, 296–98.

[3] *American Journal of Sociology*, XX, 68–97; *Primitive Society*, pp. 166–85; *University of California Publications in American Archaeology and Ethnology*, XVI, 29–45.

[4] *American Anthropologist*, N.S., XIX, 571–79.

[5] *Journal of American Folklore*, XXVII, 411–36.

[6] *Journal of the Anthropological Institute*, XVIII, 262 *et seq.*

[7] *Totemism and Exogamy*, *passim*.

[8] *Primitive Paternity; Memoirs of the American Anthropological Association*, IV, 1–90.

matrilineal, the Iroquois in the East, the Pueblos and Atapascans in the Southwest, and the Haida, Tlingit and T'simshian in the Northwest. When the evolutionists point to the importance of the maternal uncle and to such customs as the leverite and sororate among the patrilineal groups as survivals of a prior matrilineal system, the anti-evolutionists show that these culture traits can be explained in their own cultural setting without postulating a prior matrilineal stage, that there are matrilineal tribes without these culture traits, and that the presence of such traits may be the result of recent borrowing from neighboring tribes. The present status of the controversy is that, although matrilineal descent gave way to patrilineal in some parts of the world, it did not so happen in America, that there the sequence may even be reversed,[1] and that patrilineal descent may develop directly from a non-exogamous relationship without passing through an intermediate matrilineal stage.

This latter contention brings out another revision of Morgan's views. Morgan was indecisive about the existence of marriage between single pairs in the early stages of human society. He wrote, "The evidence drawn from the classificatory system tends to show that marriage between single pairs was unknown in the primitive ages of mankind," and then directly thereafter: "Instances of marriage between single pairs may have and probably did occur in all periods of man's history; but they must have been exceptional from the necessity of the case in

---

[1] ". . . . the broad general current of development indicates strongly that patrilineal institutions underlie matrilineal institutions in North America . . . ." (Kroeber, *op. cit.*, p. 575).

the primitive ages."[1] With his fundamental hypothesis
that the gens was the original type of social unit, and
was *the* marriage-regulating agency of primitive society
prior to the development of political society, and with
his religious and moral background, it is to be expected
that he would consider monogamy "the culminating institution."[2]

Lowie has, however, contended that our present
knowledge of primitive culture leads to the conclusion
that "the family is universal and omnipresent at every
stage of culture, that at a higher stage of culture it is
frequently coupled with the sib organization and at a
still higher level the sib disappears." The sib could not
have been the most primitive organization, for it is not
present precisely among the most primitive tribes and is
found, as a rule, only when horticultural or pastoral activities have partly or wholly displaced hunting as the
basis of economic existence. Morgan's cardinal principle
that kinship terms are more stable than the culture in
which they originated and that they persist long after
that culture disappears[3] here serves to refute him, for
kinship terminology linked with a sibless organization
yields no evidence of former sibs. From these facts
Lowie argues for the chronological priority of the family
and asserts: "The reversal of the traditional sequence is

---

[1] *Systems of Consanguinity*, pp. 469, 491.

[2] Lubbock had a similar view: "As we descend in the scale of civilisation,
the family diminishes, and the tribe increases in importance" (*Origin of
Civilisation*, p. 132).

[3] Karl Marx indorsed this statement and suggested that it applied as well
with reference to political, juridical, religious, and philosophical nomenclature. See F. Engels, *op. cit.*, p. 37.

one of the safest conclusions of modern ethnology."[1] Malinowski, approaching the problem from a different angle, that of a functional interpretation "of the initial situation of kinship" and of the psychological concomitants of child-rearing, substantiates this position.[2]

Controversy over the significance and implications of the kinship terms had engaged Morgan from the publication of *Systems of Consanguinity* onward. McLennan, whose solution of the origin of the exogamous gens was that it resulted from marriage by capture, insisted with some asperity that these terms had no sociological significance whatsoever but were merely terms of address or modes of salutation.[3] Morgan refuted McLennan effectively in a note on McLennan's book appended to *Ancient Society*,[4] but the controversy on whether the terms were or were not mere salutations persisted for many years.[5]

The criticism of Morgan's interpretation of the terms is now on different grounds. As has been previously suggested, Morgan regarded the terms as "survivals," indicative vestiges of antecedent social conditions. Most

[1] *Primitive Society*, pp. 147–57; Kroeber, *op. cit.*, pp. 563 *et seq.;* Goldenweiser, *Early Civilization*, pp. 235–58.

[2] *Sex and Repression in Savage Society*, pp. 263–73; in *Encyclopædia Britannica* (14th ed.), XIII, 403–9; *ibid.*, XIV, 940–50.

[3] *Studies in Ancient History* (rev. ed.), pp. 270 *et seq.*

[4] *Ancient Society*, pp. 516–31. In this note Morgan stated: "Exogamy is simply a rule of the gens, and should be stated as such." Tylor evidently overlooked this remark when he ascribed the discovery of this fact to Fison and Howitt (Tylor, *op. cit.*, p. 263).

[5] L. Fison, *Journal of Anthropological Institute*, XXIV, 369 *et seq.* Spencer and Gillen felt it necessary to state their position in *Native Tribes of Central Australia*, pp. 56–58.

contemporary ethnologists regard the terms as relationship terms expressive of status and potential relationship rather than of prior forms.[1] Lowie shows that features of kinship terminology are distributed like other ethnographic phenomena, that differences in terminology are regional, similarities within a given region being due to historical contact and diffusion, and that their distribution cannot be explained sociologically because tribes having them differ fundamentally in social organization and usage.[2] Kroeber explains kinship terms on psychological rather than sociological grounds, contending that, in view of the paucity of kinship terms as compared with possible relationships, the same word or the same stem is used to denote similar relationships. Kinship terms are therefore to him psychological recognitions of likes and differences and their expression in language.[3] Rivers, defending the sociological explanation of kinship terms, disagrees with this interpretation, contending that psychological identifications follow and are derived from customary identifications.[4] All agree that it is extremely hazardous, if not impossible, to reconstruct a form of social organization on the basis of relationship systems. In the light of contemporary discussion of kinship terms the controversy which followed Morgan and colored anthropological investigation for

[1] J. Swanton, *op. cit., passim;* W. H. R. Rivers, *op. cit.,* p. 322; A. Goldenweiser in C. E. Merriam and H. E. Barnes, *Political Theories: Recent Times,* pp. 436–45; R. H. Lowie, *Primitive Society,* pp. 61–62; R. B. Dixon, *Transactions of the New York State Archeological Association,* Vol. I.

[2] *Holmes Anniversary Volume,* pp. 293–300.

[3] *Journal of the Anthropological Institute,* XXXIX, 82–83.

[4] *Kinship and Social Organisation.*

some years as to the existence or fiction of "group marriage" has little meaning or purpose. In short, while Morgan was correct in recognizing the terms as kinship terms, his reconstruction of marriage stages on the basis of these terms was erroneous.

IV

It was Morgan's emphasis on the great importance which property relations have in determining the nature of all other aspects of social organization that brought wide recognition to *Ancient Society* in non-academic circles. This phase of the work attracted the attention and the support of Karl Marx[1] and led to Frederick Engel's book *Die Ursprung der Familie, des Privateigenthums und des Staats, im Anschluss an Lewis H. Morgan's Forschungen,* which is based on *Ancient Society* with some additional corroborative material derived from German history.[2] It is through the agency of

[1] Before reading Morgan, Marx held the family to be the initial form of social organization. He wrote in *Capital:* "Within a family and after further development within a tribe, there occurs a spontaneous division of labor . . . ." Engels appended an editorial note to this passage in the third edition: "Subsequent and exhaustive studies of the primitive condition of mankind led the author to the conclusion that the original course of development was not from the family into the tribe; but, conversely, that the tribe was the primitive and spontaneously developed form of human association based on kinship, so that the various forms of the family were the outcome of the incipient loosening of tribal bonds." *Capital* (Translation of Fourth German Edition by Eden and Cedar Paul, New York, 1929), I, 370.

[2] This book, first published in Germany in 1884, had gone into four editions by 1891 and by that time had been translated into many languages, including Italian, Rumanian, Danish, and French. The English translation of the fourth German edition, published in 1902, from which citations are made here, has had a very extensive sale, as have the other translations and the original. *Ancient Society* was translated into German in 1891 by Karl

Engel's book that Morgan's ethnological views have received the support of socialist writers all over the world. Although the majority of contemporary socialist students recognize the inadequacy of Morgan's ethnological contributions today, some are still antagonistic to any criticism of Morgan. An anomolous situation has arisen. For Morgan's evolutionary scheme of savagery, barbarism, and civilization, which contemporary anthropologists reject, has afforded a prop and rationalization for the aggressive exploitation of colonial peoples by imperialistic capitalist nations. Obviously, designations such as "savage" and "barbarian," with the implication that these people cannot change their inferior condition unaided, are easy smoke screens for aggression and have served as such. Uncritical supporters of Morgan thus defeat their own objectives by insisting on the validity of all of Morgan's hypotheses. Engels was more critical. Not only did he supplement and revise Morgan's work, but he wrote in his Preface, "The economic deductions, sufficient for Morgan's purpose but wholly inadequate for mine, were treated anew. . . . ."[1]

Morgan's views on property have four general aspects: the importance of technology in determining property relations, the evolution of property ownership from primitive communism to private property, the democratic nature of primitive communities with the

Kautsky and W. Eichhoff under the title of *Die Urgesellschaft.* August Bebel's *Die Frau und der Socialismus,* which quoted Morgan extensively, went into fifty-one editions by 1910 and was widely translated. An American translation by Daniel De Leon appeared in 1904.

[1] Preface to first edition, p. 10.

absence of slavery below the "upper status of barbarism," and the primary influence of property as an initiator of change in other aspects of social organization.

Morgan's opinion of the importance of technology in shaping property concepts, although pervading his entire discussion of property, is best expressed in his opening statement of the problem:

Each ethnical period shows a marked advance upon its predecessor, not only in the number of inventions, but also in the variety and amount of property which resulted therefrom. The multiplicity of the forms of property would be accompanied by the growth of certain regulations with reference to its possession and its inheritance. The customs upon which these rules of proprietary possession and inheritance depend, are determined and modified by the condition and progress of the social organization. The growth of property is thus closely connected with the increase of inventions and discoveries and with the improvement of social institutions which mark the several ethnical periods of human progress.[1]

This statement, denuded of its evolutionary "ethnical periods" or stages, is a clear and valid recognition of the importance of technology in influencing property relations. But Morgan stressed the evolutionary aspect of property relations:

Commencing at zero in savagery, the passion for the possession of property as the representative of accumulated subsistence, has now become dominant over the human mind in civilized races."[2]

. . . . But the property of savages was inconsiderable. Their ideas concerning its value, its desirability and its

[1] *Ancient Society*, p. 535.   [2] *Ibid.*, p. 536.

inheritance were feeble. Rude weapons, fabrics, utensils, apparel, implements of flint, stone and bone, and personal ornaments represent the chief items of property in savage life. A passion for its possession had scarcely been formed in their minds, because the thing itself scarcely existed. It was left to the then distant period of civilization to develop into full vitality that "greed of gain" (*studium lucri*) which is now such a commanding force in the human mind. Lands, as yet hardly a subject of property, were owned by tribes in common, while tenement houses were owned jointly by their occupants. Upon articles purely personal which were increasing with the slow progress of inventions, the great passion was nourishing its nascent powers. With the institution of the gens came the first great rule of inheritance, which distributed the effects of a deceased person among his gentiles.[1]

He used the Pueblos as an illustrative example of a people who know the art of pottery and agriculture and are therefore in his "middle stage of barbarism":

That any person owned lands or houses in his own right, with power to sell and convey in fee-simple to whomsoever he pleased, is not only unestablished but improbable. Their mode of owning their lands in common, or by communities of persons, their joint-tenement houses, and their mode of occupation by related families precluded the individual ownership of houses or of lands. A right to sell an interest in such lands or in such houses and to transfer the same to a stranger would break up their plan of life. The possessory right which we must suppose existed in individuals or in families was inalienable, except within the gens, and on the demise of the person would pass by inheritance to his or her gentile

[1] *Ibid.*, pp. 537–38.

heirs. Joint-tenement houses and lands in common indicate a plan of life adverse to individual ownership.[1]

Morgan did not have at hand the reliable ethnological material requisite for a thoroughgoing appraisal of this very intricate subject; he apologizes for the inadequacy of his treatment.[2] His discussion is furthermore vitiated by his evolutionary scheme. But the fact is often overlooked by his critics that he recognized that individual rights to personal property prevailed even in the simplest cultures and that, when he used the phrase "owned in common," he meant by it the gens or part of the gens, as is noted in his criticism of the Spanish accounts of Mexican land tenure:

One thing is plain, namely that these lands were owned in common by a community of persons; but one, not less essential, is not given; namely, the bond of union which held these persons together. If a gens, or a part of a gens, the whole subject would be at once understood.[3]

His belief, however, that the ownership of land among "savage" people before the invention of pottery was always tribal is erroneous. Speck was able to map out clearly defined individual hunting privileges among the northeastern Algonkians of New England and Eastern Canada;[4] Davidson has charted family hunting territories in Australia;[5] and Seligmann was able to do likewise among the Veddas of Ceylon, who not only own

[1] *Ibid.*, pp. 545–46.
[2] *Ibid.*, p. 562.   [3] *Ibid.*, p. 547.
[4] *Canadian Geological Survey Memoir, No. 70.*
[5] *American Anthropologist*, N.S., XXX, 614–81.

tracts individually and guard them jealously in that respect but transferred them.[1] Individual families held their own fishing banks, berrying patches and root-digging patches on the coast of British Columbia[2] and their fishing locations in the Puget Sound area.[3]

Morgan assumed also that property distinctions played a negligible rôle in primitive life, which was therefore essentially democratic. This generalization derived from his contact with the Iroquois is not valid even as applied to aboriginal America. Had Morgan had his field experience among the Indians of the Northwest, where a chief or man of influence and position is not the man of courage or record in war but the man of property, or even among the rude tribes of northwest California, where an avarice for wealth is found that is non-existent among the groups which he had known, he might have modified his theory.[4] Careful ethnological investigations have revealed without a doubt the existence of castes among the Natchez,[5] and that there were class distinctions and slaves on the Northwest Coast is unassailable.[6] The applicability of Morgan's theory to

[1] *The Veddas*, pp. 106–15.

[2] R. H. Lowie, *Primitive Society*, p. 212; *Yale Law Journal*, XXXVII, 551–68.

[3] Author's unpublished field notes on the Lummi Indians.

[4] Cf. A. L. Kroeber, *Transactions of XIXth Congress of Americanists*, p. 895.

[5] R. H. Lowie, *Primitive Society*, pp. 351–53. This was called to Morgan's attention by Albert Gatschet before *Ancient Society* appeared.

[6] Cf. W. C. MacLeod, *American Anthropologist*, N.S., XXX, 638–42; *ibid.*, XXXI, 89–113; E. Sapir, *Transactions of the Royal Society of Canada*, 8d Ser., IX, 355–74.

the Mexican data has already been discussed. When one leaves America and considers Polynesia and Africa, about which little was known by Morgan, the generalization is entirely erroneous. For among these groups there are sharp distinctions of caste, and slavery was a marked characteristic of the culture pattern.[1]

Morgan's emphasis on the influence of property as a factor of change of other aspects of social organization has provoked the greatest discussion. It was his opinion that originally, paternity being doubtful, property was transmitted through the mother; but that with the increase in property and increasing certainty of fatherhood, antagonism developed against the exclusion of the male owner's children, which brought about a change to descent through the father.[2] Morgan recognized the difficulty of applying his hypothesis, when he declared in regard to the Winnebagoes and related groups:

It is surprising that so many tribes of this stock should have changed descent from the female line to the male, because when first known the idea of property was substantially undeveloped, or but slightly beyond the germinating stage, and could hardly, as among the Greeks and Romans have been the operating cause.[3]

The hypothesis has proved inapplicable except in a greatly revised form. Among some groups where paternity is doubtful, as, for example, the Todas and the Torres Straits' Islanders, who do not know the relation

[1] Cf. A. M. Hocart, *Kingship;* F. Oppenheim, *The State,* pp. 345 *et seq.;* Lowie, *ibid.,* pp. 345–51.

[2] *Ancient Society,* pp. 66, 167, 222, 353, 356. Cf. *Systems of Consanguinity,* p. 492.

[3] *Ancient Society,* p. 161.

between sexual intercourse and conception, descent is nevertheless patrilineal through the man who assumes the duties of the father. As has been pointed out previously, change may sometimes have occurred from a non-exogamous society to descent through the father. Furthermore, the rule of inheritance and the rule of descent are not always the same, and a change of descent need not occur to permit a change in the transmission of property. A tribe like the Warranmunga is patronymic, and yet the legacy does not go to the relatives of the male; among the matronymic Crow and Hidatsa some kinds of property are transmitted through the mother, others through the father. The Navajo have become wealthy through sheep tended by men, which were introduced in the seventeenth century; but they have remained matrilineal.[1] The present formulation of the hypothesis of the influence of property on the change from matrilineal to patrilineal is that when, in a matrilineal society, property goes through the male and descent through the female, there is a conflict and matrilineal descent tends to give way to patrilineal.

When Morgan wrote the *League of the Iroquois*, he considered the desire for gain "one of the earliest manifestations of the progressive mind," the civilizer of the race. In *Systems of Consanguinity* he further declared it to be "the ground of his [man's] claim to civilization" and—he was just about to enter the legislature—he writes in no derogatory spirit, "Laws resolve themselves into so many agencies for the creation of protection of

[1] R. H. Lowie, *Primitive Society*, pp. 167–68; *American Journal of Sociology*, XX, 75.

property."[1] In the interim between the latter book and
Ancient Society, Morgan had had his legislative experience, and the panic of 1873 had led to personal financial
losses; and his incidental comments on the importance
of property therefore become somewhat less laudatory
and complacent. Morgan, however, writing as a member of the new capitalist class and blind to the conditions
of the workers in his day,[2] hardly merits the comment of
Engels:

Not only does he criticise civilization, the society of
production for profit, the fundamental form of human
society in a manner savoring of Fourier, but he also
speaks of a future reorganization of society in a manner
that Karl Marx might have used.[3]

He spoke as an ardent believer in the efficacy of democratic forms and a patriot of the North, nothing more,
when he wrote dramatically:

When property had become created in masses, and its
influence and power began to be felt in society, slavery
came in; an institution inviolate of all these principles,
but sustained by the selfish and delusive consideration
that the person made slave was a stranger in blood and a
captive enemy. With property, also came in gradually
the principle of aristocracy, striving for the creation of
privileged classes. The element of property, which has
controlled society to a great extent during the comparatively short period of civilization, has given mankind
despotism, imperialism, monarchy, privileged classes,
and *finally* [italics mine—B. J. S.] representative democracy. It has also made the career of civilized nations
essentially a property-making career. But when the intelligence of mankind rises to the height of the great

[1] P. 462. [2] *Supra*, pp. 31 *et seq.* [3] *Origin of the Family*, p. 26.

question of the abstract rights of property,—including the relations of property to state, as well as the rights of persons to property—a modification of the present order of things may be expected. The nature of the coming changes it may be impossible to conceive; but it seems probable that democracy, once universal in a rudimentary form and repressed in many civilized states, is destined again to become again universal and supreme.

And then lest he offend his readers in England he added apologetically:

An American, educated in the principles of democracy, and profoundly impressed with the dignity of those great conceptions which recognize the liberty, equality and fraternity of mankind, may give free expression to a preference for self government and free institutions. At the same time the equal right of every other person must be recognized to accept and approve any form of government whether imperial or monarchical that satisfies his preferences.[1]

He contended,with the corroboration of his hero, President Grant—on the basis of an inaugural address—that:

. . . . Governments over societies the most advanced are still in a transitional stage; and they are necessarily and logically moving . . . . in the direction of democracy; that form of self-government which represents and expresses the average intelligence and virtue of a free and educated people.[2]

At a time when the conditions of the workers in the anthracite coal mines had led to a bitter seven months' strike which was crushed with ruthless tactics by the operators, in the years of periodic textile strikes pro-

[1] *Ancient Society*, pp. 351–52.   [2] *Ibid.*, p. 344.

testing against starvation wages, and just prior to the great railroad strike during which President Hayes sent federal troops to aid the owners, Morgan recognized no privileged classes in the United States:

Whether this principle [aristocracy] shall live or die has been one of the great problems with which modern society has been engaged. . . . . As a question between equal rights and unequal rights, between equal laws and unequal laws, between the rights of wealth, of rank and of official position, and the power of justice and intelligence, there can be little doubt of the ultimate result. Although several thousand years have passed away without the overthrow of privileged classes *excepting in the United States* [italics mine—B. J. S.], their burdensome character upon society has been demonstrated.

His experience as state senator must have come to mind as he continued:

Since the advent of civilization, the outgrowth of property has been so immense, its forms so diversified, its uses so expanding and its management so intelligent in the interests of its owners that it has become on the part of the people an unmanageable power. The human mind stands bewildered in the presence of its own creation. The time will come, nevertheless, when human intelligence will rise to a mastery over property, and define the relations of the state to the property it protects, as well as the obligations and limits of the rights of its owners. The interests of society are paramount to individual interests, and the two must be brought into just and harmonious relations. A mere property career is not the final destiny of mankind, if progress is to be the law of the future as it has been of the past. . . . . The dissolution of society bids fair to become the termination of a career of which property is the end and aim; because such a career contains the elements of self-destruction.

His solution and prognosis is one with which Grant had expressed agreement:

Democracy in government, brotherhood in society, equality in rights and privileges, and universal education, foreshadow the next higher plane of society to which experience, intelligence and knowledge are steadily tending.[1]

Two contemporary reviews of *Ancient Society* concerned themselves especially with Morgan's views on property. The *American Socialist*, published at Oneida, New York, the organ of the Perfectionist Oneida Community, not only took occasion to stress his views of hope for a change in society but used the opportunity to advocate a "combined family," an institution which Morgan undoubtedly considered worse than Mormonism:

. . . . If then we are to expect a change in the present status of property, we must also anticipate a corresponding change in the family system, which according to Mr. Morgan is but the creature and consequence of the property system. The two must change together; and here we come again to the question, what will this change be? A careful examination of the movements of society during the period of civilization will enable the intelligent student to predict with comparative certainty the course in which the evolutionary force is acting. He will see that the tendency of the civilizing agency is operating with a constantly increasing power in the direction of combination—the aggregation and combination of interests of every kind. If the movement of property is an index in the movement of society, then the thousand combinations of property in the

[1] *Ibid.*, pp. 561–62.

form of railroads, banks, stock companies and all the multifold methods which have sprung into being with the advance of civilization, are an unerring indication of what the social status of the future is to be. If today we see in every direction, the isolated capitalist giving way before the corporation or combination of capitalists, tomorrow will be the merging of the isolated into the combined family, for one is the sequence of the other. If the isolated family was the means of developing and ripening the idea of property, the combined family is necessary to utilize and distribute it so that the highest possible benefits resulting from its increase may be realized by all.[1]

The reviewer in Frank Leslie's *Illustrated Newspaper*, after a pretense at impartiality, used the book as a support for the dominant laissez faire philosophy and as a springboard to attack the socialization program of the International Workingmen's Association (The First International), adopted at the Brussels meeting of the association in 1868, and the attempts of workers in the United States to secure protective governmental legislation. He characterized these efforts as "idle collisions with economical laws which have been approved by the experience of former generations" and continued:

. . . . Much of the so-called socialistic and communistic discussion to which we are treated in this nineteenth century and in this era of the Christian dispensation, belongs to the extinct forms of a civilization which the human race has long since left behind it in the onward march of humanity. The declaration for instance, of the International Labor Party (*sic*), at Brussels, that coal-

[1] *American Socialist* (Oneida, New York), November 15 and 22, 1877, pp. 363, 371.

mines, mines in general, soil, canals, telegraph lines, railroads etc., should belong to the State and should be worked by it in the interest of labor, or the corresponding declaration of the National Labor Party (*sic*) in our country, to the effect that the laborer needs more protection at the hands of the government, are effete dogmas which evince a radical inversion of sound economical ideas, and which fly in the face of all social progress and of all economic development down to the present time. The men who so reason (if they can be said to reason) do not know what spirit they are of when, in seeking the emancipation of labor, they would crush the freedom of the individual industry under the iron heel of the whole social organism. . . . .[1]

It was not until shortly after Morgan's death that the Social Democrats of Germany and then of other countries indorsed *Ancient Society* under Marx's and Engel's influence.

V

It is often stated that Morgan's work was neglected when not attacked during his lifetime and that only after his death was his work appreciated. The extracts from reviews and letters already given, in themselves disprove this assertion. In fact, the contrary may be said. In popular journals and newspapers *Ancient Society* received wide notice for a book on the subject with which it dealt. The *New York Times* carried two extensive favorable reviews,[2] and the *New York Tribune* was effusive in its praise.[3] The *Atlantic Monthly* declared it

[1] *Frank Leslie's Illustrated Newspaper* (New York), July 27, 1878.

[2] May 19, 1877, p. 18; August 12, 1877, p. 10.

[3] May 12, 1877.

to be a valuable contribution;[1] the *North American Review*, "by far the most important contribution to American Science that has been made for a long time."[2] The *Woman's Journal*, edited by Julia Ward Howe and Lucy Stone, carried a review by Rebecca N. Hazard characterizing Morgan's data on descent through the mother as significant in indicating "the normal conditions of society with regard to woman."[3] The *Nation* published a long expository review by Adolph Bandelier.[4] The *American Antiquarian* called it "the best book on the subject ever written."[5]

Adulatory letters from prominent Americans to Morgan were numerous, among them communications from the poet-journalist William Cullen Bryant, the popular writer Edward Howland, and from Henry Adams. Bryant urged Morgan to continue writing to earn "that immortality which no mere *belle lettres* writer can hope for in this changeful world."[6] Howland proclaimed *Ancient Society* as marking

an era in the historical study of societary development .... its method is destined to correct the historical methods now in vogue, as much as the statement of the law of gravitation did to the philosophical theories in vogue before its statement. It makes human history consistent. . . . .[7]

Henry Adams, who had previously sent Morgan a copy of his book *Anglo-Saxon Law* with the comment,

[1] September, 1877, pp. 374 *et seq.*   [4] August 9 and 16, 1877.

[2] November, 1877, pp. 589 *et seq.*   [5] I (1878), 118.

[3] November 10, 1877.   [6] Dated Buffalo, April 21, 1880.

[7] Dated Hammonton, New Jersey, July 30, 1877.

"I should be glad to be considered even an unsuccessful aspirant for honors in that field of primitive institutions where you have had so great a triumph,"[1] is thoroughgoing in his analysis of the contents of *Ancient Society:*

. . . . The position relating to our Indians interests me greatly and fills a gap which I have long wished to see filled. It must be the foundation of all future work in American historical science, and I earnestly hope that no time will be lost in pressing the same class of inquiries among the existing tribes of Indians which have come least in contact with civilization. I have lost and shall lose no opportunity to impress on our scientific men and institutions the need of a careful scientific inquiry into the laws and usages of the village Indians, and to collect in a complete form all the material which is still in existence but will not last much longer. Your influence might be decisive in organising such an undertaking. You would find active sympathy from men like Prof. Marsh, Clarence King, Alexander Agassiz, Pumpelli, and I doubt not the whole Smithsonian connection, as well as Major Powell and our various national engineering and surveying parties. The work should be started at once, and its objects defined and explained so that inquirers and travellers may understand the aims proposed. If you will take the lead in it, I believe something might be accomplished.

Of your chapters on Greek and Roman society, I am not a competent judge, this branch of the subject being one which I have always taken on trust for want of time to work it up. I feel more at home among the Germans, and here I could not fail to be struck by the want of the gentile organisation which is so essential a part of the stage of development which belonged to the early Germans. You also have observed this deficiency and have

[1] Dated Beverly Farms, Massachusetts, October 16, 1876.

commented on it. I am not yet clear in my own mind as to its causes. I can see only two possible ways of accounting for it. Either the Germans had leaped this stage, or they had not come to it. I conceive the first to have been the case, but if so, the Germans must have possessed a very remarkable instinct for the organisation of political society. This indeed is true of them in other respects, and runs through all their institutions. In these I can find not a trace of religious or priestly influence, not a sign or arbitrary power vested either in the family or the state, not even a vestige of that social degradation of women and children which is so common elsewhere. The Germans always showed a genius for reconciling liberty with law, broad political organisation with the utmost individual license. Their laws seem to me to prove that they clung to their old communal assembly as their favorite machinery of society, and by maintaining the *commune* rendered the gens and the family a mere private and politically non-existant organisation.

In connection with this subject, I noticed with pleasure a remark of yours on the influence of domestic animals in developing the Aryan race. I suspect that this is capable of further illustration in a legal sense. I strongly suspect that the oldest, or if not actually the oldest yet certainly the oldest Aryan civil procedure at law, is that procedure for the recovery of stolen cattle which is described in *Anglo-Saxon Law*. And it is obvious that the introduction of great numbers of cattle as private property must have rendered a great elaboration of legal conceptions necessary. The Aryan mind seems to have a natural bent towards it. So these complicated influences act and react in the history of human progress. Circumstances prescribe a pastoral life. The pastoral life favors the development of high physical and mental powers, as compared with a less favored state of existence. The most successful of the pastoral races find new necessities for the protection of property; they turn their practical minds to law; and all the rest follows by the logic of environment; the most capable branches of the stock, the strongest stocks grow and flower; in time we have a *Lex Salica*, a *corpus juris civilis*, and an English common law.

I regret much that Schweinfurth whose travels in Africa reveal such possibilities in barbarism, had not studied the legal side of the institutions of those immense cattle-growing tribes in Central Africa.

Of your controversy with Mr. McLennan, I say nothing. He is hopelessly wrong and I think this is conceded by pretty nearly everyone. His last edition added very bad manners to very wild theorising. You seem to have replied with propriety. Your last two chapters which are in some respects the most interesting to me, I have not yet read though I have glanced over the pages. I am thankful for the information they contain and I hope they may hereafter be capable of elaboration by you into a volume. The history of property is the history of law and the history of law is the best that man has to show.

Now that I have resigned my professorship and broken my connection with the University of Cambridge, it is doubtful I shall ever return to a practical investigation of these matters. . . . .[1]

Morgan's influence was especially great among the anthropologists of his period and that immediately following. His influence on Bandelier and his stimulation for the undertaking of research projects in the Southwest have already been mentioned. He was the nestor of American anthropologists; and all contemporary anthropologists wrote to him for counsel, sent him papers

[1] Dated Beverly Farms, Massachusetts, July 14, 1877.

for criticism, or made trips to Rochester to consult him. Among these were Horatio Hale; F. W. Putnam; L. V. Hayden; O. T. Mason; F. W. Cushing; Stephen D. Peet; the editor of the *American Antiquarian*, which was the organ of the anthropologists of his day; and J. W. Powell, the first director of the Bureau of Ethnology of the Smithsonian Institution. Powell delayed bringing out the ethnological materials which he and his collaborators had collected until he could interpret them in the light of *Ancient Society*.

I withhold all material relating to the organization of society and government among the Indians for further study and I am especially anxious to receive your new work before this subject is taken up again so that we may review the material in hand and collections of new materials in the light which will be thrown upon the subject by the publication of your researches. . . . .[1]

When the book appeared, he wrote enthusiastically:

. . . . Your book was read in one time and the first night I read until two o'clock. I shall take it into the field with me and in my leisure hours study it carefully, reading it many times. Since its reading I found that I have many facts which fall properly into the system which you have laid out: the bearing of these facts I did not understand before. Had I more fully appreciated your system, I believe I could have given you much additional data. I am fully convinced that you are right in your statement concerning the necessity that American ethnology should be studied by Americans. American languages have been thoroughly misunderstood by everyone who has written on the subject except Mr. Trumbull. American mythology is an incoherent mass

[1] Dated Washington, D.C., November 16, 1876.

of nonsense as it has hitherto been treated, especially by Europeans, but there is system of exceeding interest and beauty, and I think I shall be able soon to put it on a proper basis. I beg pardon for the egotism exhibited in this remark but I use it simply as an introduction for the following statement. After reading your book, I believe you have discovered the true system of social and governmental organization among the Indians. When I return from the field, I hope to have some materials that will interest you.[1]

Powell's paper on mythology entitled "Mythologic Philosophy" shows the influence of Morgan not only in its evolutionary classification but also in its pedantic terminology, as is shown by the following characteristic sentence:

All these tribes are found in the higher stage of savagery or the lower stages of barbarism, and their mythologies are found to be zootheistic among the lowest, physitheistic among the highest, and a great number of tribes are found to be in a transition stage, for zootheism is found to be characteristic of savagery and physitheism of barbarism using the terms as they have been used by Morgan.[2]

F. W. Putnam was a stanch admirer of Morgan, as is evidenced by some of his letters that have already been

[1] Dated Washington, D.C., May 25, 1877.

[2] *Proceedings of the American Association for the Advancement of Science, 1879*, pp. 251–78. Cf. Powell's presidential address before the Anthropological Society in 1885, in *Transactions of the Anthropological Society of Washington*, III, 173–96. Powell wrote the laudatory biographic sketch of Morgan which appeared when Morgan took the office of president of the American Association for the Advancement of Science to which he was elected in 1880 (*Popular Science Monthly*, XVIII, 114–21).

quoted. When Morgan died in 1881, Putnam wrote a biographic memoir, which concluded:

The great principles which his researches have brought out are so apparently beyond controversy that they will ever stand as the rocks against which the wild and sensational theories will be dashed, as foundations upon which to build in the further study of America in archeology and ethnology.[1]

Apparently he had been unable to resist following the tradition of obituary exaggeration, for in 1895 Putnam wrote in his diary:

In relation to Mr. Morgan: He and I were the best of friends and for several years after 1874 he was in the habit of making me a yearly visit and staying at my house for a week or more at a time, and I also visited him several times in Rochester. At these visits we always discussed anthropological matters and his views and theories were often the special subject of our discussions. During one of these visits as I distinctly remember he stated that he was living a generation too early and got founded in his beliefs before he had the facts now in hand, but that it was too late to renew his work and do it all over with the knowledge of late discoveries and that I must take the matter up and show where he had made mistakes and also what of his would stand. He died December, 1881.

Then Professor Putnam added:

Once when talking upon the subject with Mr. Dorsey I told him not to follow Morgan too closely as Morgan had himself felt that some of his views would be greatly modified.[2]

[1] *Proceedings of the American Association of Arts and Sciences*, Vol. XVII.

[2] Dated March 6, 1895.

Morgan never expressed doubts about his theories in print. His attitude (though not in his language) was like that expressed in Bandelier's letter prior to the appearance of the latter's review of *Ancient Society:*

. . . . I have tried in my review of it, which will appear in the next Nations, to break the ground for future criticisms, by endeavoring to show the true importance of the book. I suppose that a storm of indignation will arise at my utterances, for they are if anything, stronger and more aggressive than yours. It is easier to assail a Review than a Book, and I thought to throw out bait to the croakers. They will start, we can be sure of it, but they must have a pretext. An anonymous reviewer is a good victim, an author of high standing and reputation, establishing new issues, a new line of departure in some branches of science, is a dangerous man to contend with because he knows more about the subject than anyone else. In reviewing a review the colors of the public can easiest be shown. . . . . I have sent a copy of "Ancient Society" to Mexico. Besides, if time permits, I may write a review of it for a German paper. The real assault will, however, come from England, McLennan, and I suppose Markham (on South American topics) will jump upon it. From Germany, I, of course, expect sharp criticism, as anything which is not of pure teutonic make appears to them almost sacreligious. About France I would not care, if I was in your place. The French will come to terms sooner or later, as yet they are real babies in American archeology, notwithstanding the immense documentary material which they possess.[1]

Aspects of the English anthropologists' appraisal of Morgan's work have already been given. Lubbock, provoked by the unsatisfactory result of the controversy he

[1] Dated Highlands, Illinois, August 8, 1877.

had had with Morgan in *Nature* over his concept of "reformatory movements"—for Morgan, it has been seen, still is confused in this matter—while commending Morgan's abilities as a collector, minces no words in criticism:

. . . . For *Systems of Consanguinity and Affinity in the Human Family* men of science must always speak gratefully of Mr. Morgan. We have done justice I trust to Mr. Morgan's qualities as a collector. He has an eye for essential fact, he has shown perseverance and industry. Unfortunately to do good work as a speculator and a reasoner in the school of Mr. Tylor and Sir Henry Maine, a writer needs more than industry and good will. He must, at least it is highly desirable, that he should have extensive and accurate scholarship, and the command of the widest range of facts. Hegel held that the philosopher should possess encyclopedic knowledge. Now Mr. Morgan's knowledge is anything but exhaustive. Again, if a writer is to make real advances in this field, he must have a logical turn of mind and gift of arrangement. It appears to us that arrangement and logic are strangely absent from Mr. Morgan's book. Our complaint is that with inadequate equipment in every way, he has attempted a task too great for him—too great perhaps for any man—and so has darkened counsel by words without knowledge. . . . . What Morgan has added to our stock of facts will endure but his theories are doomed to rapid decay.[1]

Tylor manifested less acerbity in his criticism, part of which has already been quoted:

. . . . His scheme aims at no less than to map out in a few lines of progress the whole evolution of the family and the nation from when man was a gregarious mute to when he became a cultured republican. . . . . To state

[1] *Saturday Review*, January 5, 1878, pp. 19–21.

and to criticize as a whole such a scheme as this would take not an article but a treatise. It is best to say at once that most anthropologists who read the book will say that the author has built up a structure of theory wider and heavier than his foundations of fact will bear. His scheme will hardly be accepted as a whole, but parts of it may stand as permanent additions to the science of man, and the question is which parts. . . . .

He emphasizes one aspect of Morgan's work which later was to play an important part in his theories:

However indisposed we may be to go Morgan's length in using systems of kinship as proofs of earlier social states, we must admit that it proves itself when tested a valuable clue.[1]

Later, when he learned through Ernst Grosse that *Ancient Society* had given Morgan "a place of honour among the Fathers of German Social Democracy," he commented:

In England it is doubtful whether the artificial social scheme of Morgan's later years ever made converts to any serious extent, notwithstanding our high regard for his early work of observation and collection of facts.[2]

Herbert Spencer, in acknowledging the receipt of *Ancient Society*, wrote:

I am much obliged by the copy of your work on *Ancient Society*. It would have been useful to me had I had it earlier, when I was treating of the social composition and of family arrangements. I doubt not hereafter that when I come to deal with political organization, I shall find much matter in it of value to me.[3]

[1] *Academy*, July 20, 1878, p. 67.

[2] *Nature*, LV (November 19, 1896), 51.   [3] Dated July 19, 1877.

In France, Elie Reclus reviewed the book favorably[1] and, in transmitting the review to Morgan, expressed his admiration:

I send you by the post a number of the Journal in which I have given account to the French public of your very learned work *Ancient Society*, which makes I am convinced, an important advance in the science of Social Origins.

This first notice serves as the test of a more extended article which I have addressed to your American Review—the *Radical Review*—published by Mr. Tucker at New Bedford. I had in my former work published a critique of *Primitive Marriage* by Mr. McLennan. It was only just that I should treat with the same minuteness your work, which completes and rectifies in many points the work of the Scotch savant. I did not enter upon the discussion which has been raised between you, in which you evidently have the advantage, because, in my opinion, the essential thing and of which it is necessary to enlighten the public, rather than secondary matters, is that of maternal filiation, upon which you agree with your rival and opponent.[2]

There are few books in the history of anthropology which have had such international influence as has *Ancient Society*. Modern anthropology has found it necessary to revise many of its hypotheses but it remains as the most significant achievement of the anthropology of its period.

[1] *Feuilleton de la République Française*, November 2, 1877.

[2] Dated Hammersmith, London, December 1, 1877.

CHAPTER VII

SUMMARY

Pioneers in unploughed fields of science scrape the soil thinly, leaving the more intensive work to be done by generations that follow. They may plant some seeds of thought that later prove infertile, for their knowledge of the character of the field is imperfect. Morgan was such a pioneer. He was among the first to extend the science of social origins into the remote past. In doing so, he used an evolutionary method popular in his period but since discarded as applied to the study of culture. Divorced from its evolutionary setting, much of Morgan's work remains a permanent contribution to the yet infant science of anthropology. His Iroquois study is still considered a classic. His discovery of the character of kinship systems was epoch-making; and, irrespective of his interpretations and his arrangement, his compilation of the data in this field has proved to be a lasting storehouse of fact for all later anthropologists. He shares with Maine the honor of having made and substantiated the discerning distinction between kinship affiliation and territorial affiliation, which is still applicable in a modified form. His suggestive judgment of the influence of technology in determining property relations and his intelligent insight into the importance of property as an initiator of change in other aspects of social organization are clouded, but not obscured, by his inadequate discussion and erroneous application of these principles. Morgan was not the "discoverer of the law of social progress," as he is boldly characterized on his commemorative tablet at Wells College in Aurora, New York. But he stands among the notable founders of anthropology, as one who, in spite of limited scientific equipment, a meager library, and a scanty factual foundation upon which to build, through his own persistent efforts was able to contribute much to the methodology and source material of that science.

BIBLIOGRAPHY

I. PUBLISHED AND UNPUBLISHED WRITINGS OF
LEWIS HENRY MORGAN

1840. "Non-Resistance." Address before Aurora Lyceum, April 7, 1840. 29 pp. Unpublished.[1]
1841. "Geology." Address, Aurora, June 7, 1841. 25 pp. Unpublished.
"History and Genius of the Grecian Race." Address before Cayuga Academy, November 8, 1841. 34 pp. Unpublished.
1842. "Temperance." Address, Tuppers Corners, August 21, 1842. 21 pp. Unpublished.
1843. "Address by Skenandoah on the Second Anniversary of the *We-yo Hao-de-za-da-na Ha-de-naw-saw-nee.*" Aurora, August 9, 1843. 24 pp. Unpublished.
"Aristomenes the Messenian." By "Aquarius." *Knickerbocker*, January, 1843, pp. 25–30.
"Mind or Instinct, an Inquiry Concerning the Manifestation of Mind by the Lower Orders of Animals." By "Aquarius." *Ibid.*, November–December, 1843, pp. 414–20, 507–15.
"Temperance." Address, Geneva, May 5, 1843; Spring Port, May 14, 1843. 27 pp. Unpublished.
"Temperance." Address, Scipio, December 10, 1843. 29 pp. Unpublished.
"Thoughts at Niagara." By "Aquarius." *Knickerbocker*, September 1843,, pp. 193–96.

[1] Unless otherwise indicated, all unpublished material is in the Library of the University of Rochester, Rochester, New York.

1844. "Address by Skenandoah before the *Gue-u-gweh-o-noh.*" Aurora, April 17, 1844. 17 pp. Unpublished.

"Form of Inindianation of Grand Order of the Iroquois." August 9, 1844. 2 pp. Unpublished.

"Vision of *Kar-is-ta-gi-a,* a Sachem of Cayuga." By "Aquarius." *Knickerbocker,* September, 1844, pp. 238–45.

1845. "Census Schedules of Warriors of the New Confederacy of the Iroquois: Cayuga Nation— White Deer Tribe; Cayuga Nation—Wolf Tribe; Oneida Nation—Two Tribes; Seneca Nation—Turtle Tribe; Seneca Nation—White Deer Tribe; Seneca Nation—Wolf Tribe." Unpublished.

"Doings and Facts Obtained at the Grand Council of the Iroquois, Held at the Council House of the Senecas on the Reservation in Genesee County, New York, October 1, 2, and 3, 1845." 30 pp. Unpublished.

"Onondaga Nation: Their New Year's Feast, the Sacrifice of the White Dog, Their Dances, Their Present Condition, the School Lately Established among Them, with a Few Reflections." Address before the Order of the Iroquois. 16 pp. 1845? Unpublished.

"Political Organization of the Onondaga Nation." Address before the Order of the Iroquois. 15 pp. 1845? Unpublished.

"Special Form of Inindianation." Adopted at the Monthly Council of the Turtle Sachemship of the Senecas, "Moon of *Te-ah-no-at-nah,* 7th day, 1845." 3 pp. Unpublished.

1846. "Constitution of the New Confederacy of the Iroquois," adopted at the Fourth Annual

Council, "Moon of *Sr-is-gak-nah*, 13th day, 1846." 6 pp. Unpublished.

"Constitutional Resolution and Rules and Orders of the Council of the Seneca Nation—Turtle Tribe." May 18, 1846. 3 pp. Unpublished.

"Geography and Trails of the *Ho-de-no-sau-nee.*" Address by "Skenandoah" before the Council of Delegates of the New Confederacy of the Iroquois. Aurora, New York, August 13, 1846. 56 pp. Unpublished.

"Government and Institutions of the Iroquois." Address by "Skenandoah" before the Turtle Tribe of the *Nun-da-wa-ro-noh* at the falls of the Genesee before the monthly council. November 7, 1845.

Same, as "Constitutional Government of the Six Nations." Read before New York Historical Society, April 7, 1846. 33 pp. In Reynolds Library, Rochester. Unpublished.

"Indian Trail from the Central Council Fire at Onondaga to the Council Fire at Buffalo Creek." 3 pp. 1846? Unpublished.

"Laws of the New Confederacy of the Iroquois," adopted at the Fourth Annual Council. Aurora, August 14, 1846. Unpublished.

"Seneca Chiefs Who Signed the Treaty by Which They Conveyed Away Their Lands in Western New York." 1846? Unpublished.

1847. "Letters on the Iroquois, Addressed to Albert Gallatin, President of New York Historical Society." By "Skenandoah." *American Review*, Letters 1–3, Vol. V, pp. 177–90; Letters 4–8, V, 242–57; Letters 9–11, V, 447–61; Letters 12–13, VI, 477–90; Letter 14, VI, 626–33.

Same. In N. B. Craig's *Olden Time*. Pittsburgh, 1848. Reprinted Robt. Clark & Co., 1876 (first 11 letters only).

"On the Territorial Limits, Geographical Names, and Trails of the Indians." Address before the New York Historical Society, May 4, 1847. 52 pp. and 2 folded maps. In the archives of the New York Historical Society. Unpublished.

1849. "Communications Concerning the Indian Collection and Reports on Articles." *New York State Museum Report*, Rept. 2, for 1848 (1849), pp. 81–91; Rept. 3, for 1849 (rev. ed. 1850), pp. 59–95; Rept. 5, for 1851 (1852), pp. 67–117.

Same. Abridged in *Stryker's American Register*, Vol. IV (July, 1850).

Same. Under title "List of Articles Manufactured by Indians of Western New York and Canada West." *Catalogue of Cabinet of Natural History*, Albany, 1853.

1851. *League of the Ho-de-no-sau-nee or Iroquois.* Rochester: Sage & Co.; New York: M. H. Newman Co., 1851.

Same. London: Chapman, 1851.

Same. New edition edited and annotated by Herbert M. Lloyd. New York: Dodd, 1902.

Same. New edition in one volume. New York: Dodd, 1904.

Same. Revised edition in one volume. New York: Dodd, 1922.

1852. *Diffusion against Centralization.* Lecture delivered before Rochester Athenaeum and Mechanics Association, January 6, 1852. Rochester: Dewey, 1852.

Laws of Consanguinity and Descent of the Iroquois. Rochester, 1852.

1853. "Athenian Democracy." Review of F. Boekh, *Public Economy of the Athenians* (New York quarterly), October, 1853, pp. 341–67.

1854. "The Andes." Address before "The Club," December 19, 1854. 15 pp. Unpublished.

1856. *Narrative of the Life of Mary Jemison: Deh-he-wa-mis.* By J. E. Seaver. 4th ed. Edited with geographical and explanatory notes by Morgan. New York: Miller; Rochester: Dewey, 1856. Morgan is responsible for publisher's note dated Rochester, March, 1856, pp. 7–9, and also notes in Appendix V, pp. 300–312. All subsequent editions of this work carry the notes written by Morgan.

"Laws of Descent of the Iroquois." *American Association for the Advancement of Science, Proceedings of Eleventh Meeting* (Montreal, August, 1856), Sec. 2, pp. 132–48.

Same. Cambridge, Massachusetts, 1858.

1857. "Animal Psychology." Address before "The Club," April 7, 1857. 35 pp. Unpublished.

1858. "Laws of Descent of the Iroquois." Address before "The Club," February 23, 1858. 35 pp. Unpublished.

"Origin and Results of 'The Club.'" Read October 5, 1858. 14 pp. Unpublished.

1859. "Agassiz. Theory of the Diverse Origin of the Human Race." Address before "The Club," May 16, 1859. 25 pp. Unpublished.

Circular letters in regard to the possibility of identifying the system of consanguinity of the North American Indians with that of certain peoples of Asia. Rochester, New York, January, 1859; October 1, 1859.

"Indian Mode of Bestowing Names." *American Association for the Advancement of Science, Proceedings of 13th Meeting* (Springfield, Massachusetts, August, 1859), pp. 340–42.

"System of Consanguinity of the Red Race in Its Relations to Ethnology." Address before the American Association for the Advancement of Science, Springfield, August, 1859. 23 pp. Unpublished.

1860. "Circular in Reference to Degrees of Relationship among Different Nations." *Smithsonian Institution Miscellaneous Collections*, Vol. II, Art. 10, p. 34.

"Discussion of the Feasibility of Organizing a Rochester Academy of Science," Address before "The Club," March 27, 1860. 10 pp. Unpublished.

1861. "Suggestions for Proposed Ethnological Map of North America." *Smithsonian Institution Annual Report, 1861.* 37th Congress, 2d sess. *House Misc. Docs.*, LXXVII, 397–98.

"Memoir of Calvin Hudson, Jr." Address before "The Club," November 5, 1861. 36 pp. Unpublished.

Same. Address before the Rochester Historical Society, March 31, 1862. 36 pp. Unpublished.

1868. *American Beaver and His Work:* Philadelphia: Lippincott, 1868.

"Conjectural Solution of the Origin of the Classificatory System of Relationship." *American Academy of Arts and Science, Proceedings*, VII (1865–68), 436–77. Read February 11, 1868.

1869. "Indian Migrations." *North American Review*, CIX (October, 1869), 391–442; CX (January, 1870), 33–82.

Same. In W. W. Beach's *Indian Miscellany* (Albany: Munsell, 1877), pp. 158–257.

Same. Part IV of *Systems of Consanguinity*.

"Seven Cities of Cibola." *North American Review*, CXVIII (April, 1869), 457–98.

1870. "Systems of Consanguinity and Affinity of the Human Family." *Smithsonian Institution Contribution to Knowledge*, Vol. XVII (1870), Art. 2.

Same. Reprinted. Smithsonian Institution, 1871.

1871. "Stone and Bone Implements of the Arickarees." *New York State Museum Reports*, Rept. 21, for 1867 (1871), pp. 25–46.

1872. "Australian Kinship, from the Original Memoranda of Rev. Lorimer Fison." *American Academy of Arts and Science, Proceedings*, VIII (March 12, 1872), 412–38.

"Genesis of Human Development." Original draft. July 18, 1872. 15 pp. Unpublished.

1874. "Architecture of the American Aborigines." Address before American Association for the Advancement of Science, Portland, 1874. Unpublished.

1875. "Arts of Subsistence." *American Association for the Advancement of Science, Proceedings of 24th Meeting* (Detroit, 1875), pp. 274–82.

"Ethnical Periods." *Ibid.*, pp. 266–74.

1876. "Factory System for Indian Reservations." *Nation*, XXIII (July 27, 1876), 58–59.

"Houses of the Mound Builders." *North American Review*, CXXIII (July, 1876), 60–85.

"Hue and Cry against the Indians." *Nation*, XXIII (July 20, 1876), 40–41.

"Montezuma's Dinner." *North American Review*, CXXII, 265–308.

"Moral and Political Condition of Europe and America." 43 pp. Unpublished.

1877. *Ancient Society; or, Researches in the Lines of Human Progress from Savagery through Barbarism to Civilization.* New York: Holt, 1877; reissued, 1878; new ed., reprint, 1907.

Same. London: Macmillan, 1877.

Same. Chicago: Charles H. Kerr & Co. Nine editions since 1909.

Same. Translated into German by Karl Kautsky and W. Eichhoff under title *Die Urgesellschaft* (1891).

Same. Translated into Russian by Kudriavskii Dmitrii Nikolaevich, St. Petersburg, 1900.

Same. Translated into many other languages, including Japanese.

1878. "Architecture of the American Indian." In *Johnson's New Universal Cyclopaedia*, I (New York, 1878), 217–29.

"Indian Question in 1878." *Nation*, XXVII, 332–33. Letter dated November 22, 1878.

"Migrations of American Aborigines." In *Johnson's New Universal Cyclopaedia*, III (New York, 1878), 481–84.

1880. Introduction to *Kamilaroi and Kurnai*, pp. 1–30, by Lorimer Fison and A. W. Howitt. Melbourne and Sidney: Robertson, 1880.

"On the Ruins of a Stone Pueblo on the Animas River in New Mexico; with a Ground Plan." *Peabody Museum of American Archeology and Ethnology, 12th Report* (Cambridge, 1880), II, No. 3, 536–56.

"Response as President of the American Academy for the Advancement of Science to Mayor F. O. Prince's welcome to Boston." *American Association for the Advancement of Science, Proceedings of 29th Meeting* (Boston, 1880), pp. 743–45.

Same. In *Boston Daily Advertiser*, August 26, 1880.

"Study of the Houses of the American Aborigines with Suggestions for the Exploration of the Ruins of New Mexico, Arizona, the Valley of

the San Juan and in Yucatan and Central
America." *Archaeological Institute of America,
1st Annual Report* (Cambridge, 1880), Appendix, pp. 27–80.

Same. Abridged in J. W. Powell's *Introduction to
the Study of Indian Languages* (2d ed.; Washington: Government Printing Office, 1880), pp.
21–22.

1881. "Letter to the American Association for the Advancement of Science." *American Association
for the Advancement of Science, Proceedings of
30th Meeting* (Cincinnati, August, 1881), p. 365.

"Houses and House Life of American Aborigines." *Contributions to North American Ethnology*, United States Geographical and Geological Survey of the Rocky Mountain Region
(J. J. Powell, director), No. 4. Washington,
1881.

II. SELECTED REFERENCES

BACHOFEN, J. J. *Das Mutterrecht.* Stuttgart, 1861.

BANCROFT, HUBERT H. *Early American Chroniclers.*
San Francisco, 1883.

BANDELIER, ADOLPH. "On the Art of War and Mode of
Warfare of the Ancient Mexicans." *Report of the Peabody Museum*, X (1877), 95–166.

———. "On the Distribution and Tenure of Land and
Customs in Respect to Inheritance among the Ancient
Mexicans." *Ibid.*, XI (1878), 385–448.

———. "On the Social Organization and Mode of Government of the Ancient Mexicans." *Ibid.*, XII (1879),
557–699.

———. *Romantic School of American Archeology.* 1885.

BEAUCHAMP, WILLIAM M. "Aboriginal Communal Life
in America," *American Antiquarian and Oriental
Journal*, IX (1887), 343–50.

BEBEL, AUGUST. *Woman under Socialism.* Translated from 33d German edition by Daniel De Leon. New York, 1904.

BOAS, FRANZ. *Mind of Primitive Man.* New York, 1911.

————. "America and the Old World," *XXIᵉ Congrès International des Américanistes* (1924), pp. 21–28.

BRIFFAULT, ROBERT. *Mothers.* 3 vols. New York, 1927.

CASS, LEWIS. "Aboriginal Structures." *North American Review,* CIX·(October, 1840), 396–433.

CRAPSEY, ALGERNON S. "Lewis Henry Morgan—Scientist, Philosopher, Humanist." *Rochester Historical Society, Publication Fund Series,* Vol. II. Rochester, 1923.

CUNOW, HEINRICH. *Verwandtschafts-Organisationen der Australneger.* Stuttgart, 1894.

————. *Zur Urgeschichte der Ehe und Familie.* Stuttgart, 1912.

DARWIN, CHARLES. *Descent of Man.* New York, 1872.

DAVIDSON, D. S. "Family Hunting Territory in Australia." *American Anthropologist,* N.S., XXX (1928), 614–31.

DE HASS, W. "The Mound-Builders: An Inquiry into Their Assumed Southern Origin." *Smithsonian Miscellaneous Collections,* XXV, 55–57.

DEWEY, CHARLES. "Personal Reminiscences of Lewis H. Morgan." *Rochester Historical Society, Publication Fund Series,* Vol. II. Rochester, 1923.

ENGELS, FREDERICK. *Origin of the Family, Private Property and the State.* Translation of 4th German edition. Chicago, 1902.

FISKE, JOHN. "Colonization of the New World." *History of All Nations,* Vol. XXI (New York, 1905).

————. *Discovery of America.* Boston, 1892.

FISON, LORIMER. "Classificatory System of Relationship." *Journal of the Anthropological Institute,* XXIV (1895), 369 *et seq.*

FISON, LORIMER, and HOWITT, A. W. *Kamilaroi and Kurnai.* Melbourne and Sydney. Robertson, 1880.

FRAZER, JAMES G. *Totemism and Exogamy.* 4 vols. London, 1910.

GALLATIN, ALBERT. "Notes on the Semi-Civilized Nations of Mexico, Yucatan and Central America." *Transactions of the American Ethnological Society, 1852* (New York), Vol. I.

GILCHRIST, DONALD B. "Lewis Henry Morgan: His Gifts to the University of Rochester and a Bibliography of His Works." *Rochester Historical Society, Publication Fund Series,* Vol. II. Rochester, 1923.

GOLDENWEISER, ALEXANDER A. "Anthropological Theories of Political Origins." In Merriam, Charles E., and Barnes, Harry E., *Political Theories: Recent Times,* pp. 436–45. New York, 1924.

———. *Culture. The Diffusion Controversy.* New York, 1927.

———. *Early Civilization.* New York, 1922.

———. "Social Organization of the American Indians." *Journal of American Folklore,* XXVII (1914), 411–36.

GUMPLOWICZ, LUDWIG. *Der Rassenkampf.* Innsbruck, 1883.

HADDON, A. C. *History of Anthropology.* London, 1910.

HART, CHARLES H. *Memoir of Lewis H. Morgan of Rochester, New York. Address before the Numismatic and Antiquarian Society of Philadelphia, May 4, 1882.* Philadelphia, 1883.

HARTLAND, E. SIDNEY. "Matrilineal Kinship and the Question of Its Priority." *Memoirs of the American Anthropological Association,* IV (1917), 1–90.

———. *Primitive Paternity.* 2 vols. London, 1909.

HOCART, A. M. *Kingship.* Oxford, 1927.

HOLMES, W. H. "Biographical Memoir of Lewis Henry Morgan, 1818–1881." Address before the National Academy of Science, November 20, 1907. *Na-*

tional Academy of Science, Biographical Memoirs, VI (1909), 219–39.

———. Same. *Rochester Historical Society, Publication Fund Series*, Vol. II. Rochester, 1923.

HOWITT, A. W. "Notes on Australian Class Systems." *Journal of the Anthropological Institute*, XIII (1883), 499–504.

HOWITT, A. W., and FISON, LORIMER. *See* Fison, Lorimer.

KELLER, A. *See* Sumner, W. G.

KROEBER, A. L. "Classificatory Systems of Relationship." *Journal of the Anthropological Institute*, XXXIX (1909), 77–83.

———. "Matrilineate Again." *American Anthropologist*, N.S., XIX (1917), 571–79.

LENIN, NIKOLAI. *State and Revolution.* New York, 1917.

LESSER, ALEXANDER. "Kinship Origins in the Light of Some Distributions," *American Anthropologist*, N.S., XXXI (1929), 710–30.

LOWIE, ROBERT H. *Are We Civilized?* New York, 1929.

———. *Culture and Ethnology.* New York, 1917.

———. "Historical and Sociological Interpretation of Kinship Terminologies." *Holmes Anniversary Volume*, pp. 293–300. Washington, 1916.

———. "Incorporeal Property in Primitive Society." *Yale Law Journal*, XXXVII (1928), 551–63.

———. "Matrilineal Complex." *University of California Publications on American Archaeology and Ethnology*, XVI (1919), 29–45.

———. "Note on Relationship Terminologies." *American Anthropologist*, N.S., XXX (1928), 263–67.

———. "Origin of the State." *Freeman*, V, 440–42, 465–67. New York, 1926.

———. *Origin of the State.* New York, 1927.

———. *Primitive Society.* New York, 1920.

———. "Social Organization." *American Journal of Sociology*, XX (1914), 68–97.

LUBBOCK, JOHN. *Origin of Civilisation.* London, 1870.

McILVAINE, J. H. "Funeral Address of L. H. Morgan." In L. H. Morgan, *League of the Iroquois* (Lloyd ed., 1904), pp. 167 *et seq.*

——. Same. *Rochester Historical Society, Publication Fund Series,* Vol. II. Rochester, 1923.

McLENNAN, J. F. *Primitive Marriage.* London, 1865.

——. *Studies in Ancient History.* London, 1876. New ed. London, 1886.

MacLEOD, WILLIAM C. "Economic Aspects of Indigenous American Slavery." *American Anthropologist,* N.S., XXX (1928), 632–50.

——. "Origin of Servile Labor Groups." *Ibid.,* XXXI (1929), 89–113.

——. *Origin of the State.* Philadelphia, 1924.

MAINE, HENRY. *Ancient Law.* London, 1861.

——. *Lectures on the Early History of Institutions.* London, 1875.

MALINOWSKI, BRONISLAW. *Crime and Custom in Savage Society.* New York, 1926.

——. *Father in Primitive Psychology.* New York, 1927.

——. "Kinship." *Encyclopædia Britannica* (14 ed.; New York), XIII, 403–9.

——. "Marriage." *Ibid.,* XIV, 940–50.

——. *Sex and Repression in Savage Society.* New York, 1927.

——. *Sexual Life of Savages in Northwestern Melanesia.* New York, 1929.

MARETT, R. R. *Diffusion of Culture.* Cambridge, 1927.

MARX, KARL. *Capital.* Translation. New York, 1929.

Morgan Centennial Celebration, Wells College, Aurora, New York. Being an account of the proceedings and the text of the addresses delivered by R. B. Dixon, K. D. MacMillan, and A. C. Parker. *New York State Archaeological Association, Lewis H. Mor-*

gan Chapter, Researches and Transactions, Vol. I, No. 3. 31 pp. Rochester, 1919.

MULLER-LYER, F. *Evolution of Modern Marriage.* Translation. New York, 1930.

———. *History of Social Development.* Translation. New York, 1921.

OPPENHEIMER, FRANZ. *The State.* Translation. New York, 1926.

POWELL, J. W. "From Savagery to Barbarism." *Transactions of the Anthropological Society of Washington,* III (1888), 173–96.

———. "Mythologic Philosophy." *American Association for the Advancement of Science, Proceedings, 1879,* pp. 251–78.

———. "Sketch of Lewis H. Morgan." *Popular Science Monthly,* XVIII (1880), 114–21.

PUTNAM, F. W. "Sketch of Hon. Lewis Henry Morgan." *Proceedings of the American Association for Arts and Science, 1882,* Vol. XVII.

RADIN, PAUL. "The Sources and Authenticity of the History of the Ancient Mexicans." *University of California Publications on American Archaeology and Ethnology,* XVII (1920), 1–150.

RIVERS, W. H. R. *Kinship and Social Organisation.* London, 1914.

———. "On the Origin of the Classificatory System of Relationships." *Anthropological Essays Presented to E. B. Tylor,* pp. 309–323. 1907.

———. *Social Organization.* New York, 1924.

SAPIR, E. "Social Organization of West Coast Tribes." *Transactions of the Royal Society of Canada,* 3d ser., IX (1916), 355–74.

SCHURTZ, H. *Alterklassen und Männerbunde.* Berlin, 1902.

SEILLIERE, ERNEST. "Lewis H. Morgan et la philosophie Marxiste de l'histoire." *Revue germanique,* Vol. III (1907).

SELIGMANN, C. G., and SELIGMANN, B. Z. *The Veddas.* Cambridge, 1911.

SMITH, G. ELLIOTT, and OTHERS. *Culture. The Diffusion Controversy.* New York, 1927.

SPECK, F. G. "Family Hunting Territories." *Memoirs of the Canadian Geological Survey,* No. 70. Ottawa, 1915.

SPIER, LESLIE. "Distribution of Kinship Systems in North America." *University of Washington Publications in Anthropology,* I, 71–88. Seattle, 1925.

SPINDEN, HERBERT J. "Formal Inbreeding in Human Society." *Eugenics, Genetics and the Family.* Baltimore, 1923.

STERN, BERNHARD J. "Selections from the Letters of Lorimer Fison and A. W. Howitt to Lewis Henry Morgan." *American Anthropologist,* N.S., XXXII (1930), 257–79, 419–53.

SUMNER, W. G., and KELLER, A. *Science of Society.* 4 vols. New Haven, 1927.

SWANTON, J. "Social Organization of American Tribes." *American Anthropologist,* N.S., VII (1905), 662–73.

THOMAS, N. W. *Kinship Organisation and Group Marriage in Australia.* Cambridge, 1906.

TOZZER, ALFRED M. *Social Origins and Social Continuities.* New York, 1925.

TYLOR, EDWARD B. "On a Method of Investigating the Development of Institutions." *Journal of the Anthropological Institute,* XVIII (1889), 262 *et seq.*

WALLIS, WILSON D. *Culture and Progress.* New York, 1930.

WATERMAN, T. T. "Bandelier's Contribution to the Study of Ancient Mexican Social Organization." *University of California Publications on American Archaeology and Ethnology,* XII (1917), 249–83.

WESTERMARCK, EDWARD. *History of Human Marriage.* 3 vols. London, 1921.

WISSLER, C. *Introduction to Social Anthropology.* New York, 1929.

INDEX

INDEX

INDEX 221